ME, MYSELF & GOD

A THEOLOGY OF MINDFULNESS

RABBI JEFF ROTH

For People of All Faiths, All Backgrounds
JEWISH LIGHTS Publishing
Woodstock, Vermont

Me, Myself & God:
A Theology of Mindfulness

2016 Quality Paperback Edition, First Printing
© 2016 by Jeff Roth

Unless otherwise specified, all biblical quotations are taken from *The Five Books of Moses*, translated by Everett Fox, The Schocken Bible, vol. 1 (New York: Schocken Books, 1995). Fox uses "YHWH" and lowercase pronouns for God, which have been edited here for consistency with the rest of the text. Excerpt from Daniel Matt, *Zohar: The Book of Enlightenment* (Mahwah, NJ: Paulist Press, 1983) used by permission.

Library of Congress Cataloging-in-Publication Data
Names: Roth, Jeff, author.
Title: Me, myself and God : a theology of mindfulness / by Jeff Roth.
Description: Woodstock, VT : Jewish Lights Publishing, a division of LongHill
     Partners, Inc., [2016] | Includes bibliographical references.
Identifiers: LCCN 2016016211| ISBN 9781580238755 (pbk.) |
     ISBN 9781580238779 (ebook)
Subjects: LCSH: Spiritual life—Judaism. | Meditation—Judaism.
Classification: LCC BM723 .R653 2016 | DDC 296.7—dc23 LC record available at
     https://lccn.loc.gov/2016016211

10   9   8   7   6   5   4   3   2   1

Manufactured in the United States of America
Cover design: Jenny Buono
Cover art: © sommthink/Shutterstock
Interior design: Tim Holtz

For People of All Faiths, All Backgrounds
Jewish Lights Publishing
A Division of LongHill Partners, Inc.
Sunset Farm Offices, Route 4, P.O. Box 237
Woodstock, VT 05091
Tel: (802) 457-4000 Fax: (802) 457-4004
www.jewishlights.com

This book is dedicated with love to
Rabbi Zalman Schachter-Shalomi *z"l*

Contents

Introduction

It is with great excitement that I entrust this book to you, dear reader. Over the course of the last two decades I have come to understand that many of our human existential struggles stem from the sense of separation that comes from a confused and fragmented view of reality. With this book I hope to shed some light on the causes and workings of this predicament. More importantly, it is my hope that this book will offer you the insights and practices necessary to overcome this sense of separation and reconnect you with a more wholesome, harmonious flow of life. We all are integral aspects of what I call the "Unfolding of Being," and as human beings we are called by that reality to the enterprise of awakening our heart/mind.

But mixed into my excitement is also some doubt regarding the possibility of passing on what I have learned. After all, much of it was initially received through direct contact with inspirational teachers and their practices. Their teachings were then incorporated into two decades of personal reflection. How can a book possibly transmit this kind of inspiration? How can it impart a wisdom that is in essence experiential and not conceptual? And how can I connect to you, dear reader? It is my deepest wish that we all realize our spiritual inheritance by cultivating a contemplative practice, one that truly awakens us to the Unfolding of Being and our place in it and that arouses our hearts to recognize their natural state of love and compassion.

During my college years, I became committed to social justice and searched for a lifestyle that would support my ideas. I found inspirational Jewish teachers who presented an approach to Jewish practices that was congruent with the pursuit of justice and nurturance for all beings. This eventually led to my decision to become a rabbi. Even back then, I think, I had a keen sense of the suffering that comes from self-centered and self-serving actions. But I didn't really have a contemplative practice, and I certainly didn't have the spiritual insight necessary to fully grasp the depth of what caused our plight. That only began to change when I met Reb Zalman Schachter-Shalomi. It was his teachings and his introduction to meaningful forms of prayer that sparked the beginnings of a spiritual awakening in me. Reb Zalman passed away during the final editing process of this work, and so I dedicate this book to his memory.

We met for the first time thirty-five years ago. My *havurah* (spiritual community) had invited Reb Zalman for a weekend of teachings, and he chose to present us with a central tenet of the Baal Shem Tov (Master of the Good Name), the eighteenth-century Polish founder of Hasidic Judaism. "Everything is God and nothing but God," he told us. The Baal Shem Tov (also known as the Besht, an acronym of his name) emphasized this teaching as the core of his revival movement, and emphasized a religious practice that could lead to direct experience of the Divine.

That weekend was my first encounter with Jewish mysticism. Reb Zalman invited us to share our deepest questions about God and spiritual life. He sat there and listened quietly to about ten of us before he began to speak. I remember his talk was a brilliant discourse that wove in all the different questions asked. But what really made a deep impression on me was how all of the questions had a single answer: the nature of the Divine. Everything, Reb Zalman pointed out, was a manifestation of the Divine, was part of the Oneness of Being. Ever since, anytime I reflect on the nature of a particular aspect of reality, I think, "Oh, that too is part of the Everything that is God, the Everything that God is." It was an important opening for me and marked the moment in which I became fully engaged by a God-centered focus for my Jewish spirituality.

As powerful as this lesson was, it took me another few years before I really started a contemplative practice of my own. A decade after I met Reb Zalman, my partner, Rabbi Joanna Katz, and I founded Elat Chayyim, a Jewish retreat center dedicated to progressive Jewish spirituality. We were about two years into this project when we invited mindfulness teacher Sylvia Boorstein to lead a meditation retreat at Elat Chayyim. Sylvia's teachings on the nature of mind and how to work with it using mindfulness meditation deeply resonated with me. The practice of mindfulness is to bring clear, balanced, nonjudgmental, awakened attention to the truth of what is unfolding each moment. And the Truth of What Is Unfolding Each Moment (you will notice I capitalized this phrase) is all God and nothing but God from a mystical Jewish perspective. I immediately knew that mindfulness was the practice and approach I needed to add to my spiritual path. The practices and insights Sylvia shared with us on that retreat provided an expansion of perspective to me that was as immediate and profound as Reb Zalman's had been. Moreover, in starting the practice, I soon realized that for me mindfulness perfectly integrated with the mystical truth that "everything is God and nothing but God." So for the years to follow I committed my spiritual practice to an exploration of how each moment fits into the pattern of God's nature or "Being Unfolding." Reclaiming language referring to the Divine within this context, I realized, offered an enrichment to classical mindfulness practice that is not generally taught in connection to theology. When paying attention in the present moment is experienced and recognized as a moment of God realization, I want to refer to these experiences with words that are in essence names for God. Since I experience being loved as being loved by the Divine I use "Love" as a name for God. When I feel that the love being expressed through me when I attend to various aspects of life is the Divine operating through me then I experience "Loving Attention" as another synonym for God. (In Jewish mysticism there are many names for God, illustrating the mystical understanding that Oneness includes everything. In fact, the Torah in its entirety is considered a single name of God. Throughout this book, I will use capital letters to point to the various God names.) This richness, which I believe has something to offer to both Judaism and classical mindfulness, is the focus of this book.

Soon after beginning my journey, my contemplative path gave me a sense of integration with the Flow of All Being, and I saw how contemplative practice could lead us all to experience the Oneness of Inter-being. It is the thinking mind, with its beliefs, opinions, and concepts, that creates the illusion of separateness. Loving Attention is the way to intuit an undivided reality in which everything is unfolding. I began to study the Torah from this perspective, and I realized that the book of Genesis can be read as a profound description of the arising of human consciousness and the sense of separation that comes from it. Particularly, the origin of language and conceptual thinking led to—and continues to lead to—a sense of disconnectedness, alienation, and loneliness. In the Torah, this separation is depicted as the expulsion of human beings from the Garden of Eden. From the time of that expulsion forward, the Torah depicts the situation of human beings as continually declining until its nadir, which is depicted as slavery in Egypt. This is a vivid image of how desperate the human condition can and has become. But in the book of Exodus, which tells the story of deliverance from Egypt, the Torah hints at what is necessary to turn this separation and alienation around, how to liberate ourselves from our self-inflicted slavery by creating a new relationship with God. Of course, the Torah is a rich and multilayered text that can be read in many different ways, but one clear lesson for me is how the arising of human consciousness and its nature leads to a sense of separation and creates suffering. Equally clear, though, is that we can learn from it a path of liberation, the path of holiness.

Underlying my spiritual practice are the perennial questions: Who am I? What is the nature of the Divine? How do the two overlap? It is entirely possible that these questions are central to most spiritual traditions. This book offers my reflections on the subject, and I hope to show how the practice of mindfulness elucidates the underlying lessons of Genesis and Exodus on these questions. Even more importantly, mindfulness provides a path to liberation (from Egypt or the delusion of separateness), and this book invites you to partake in the journey. It's a journey that begins by fostering Loving Attention to the truth of how things are, moment by moment. This journey can lead us to the fruits of realization: wisdom, the cultivating of compassion, and the expression of loving-kindness.

In my first book, I told a little story I heard from Reb Zalman. One day, his daughter Shalvi, who was about seven at the time, came to him. "Abba," she said, "you know when you are asleep and dreaming, it all seems so real; but when you wake up, you realize that it was just a dream. I am wondering: when you are awake, do you think you could wake up even more and realize that this is a dream, too?" I believe that this waking up is indeed not only possible but our birthright. We all have the innate capacity to overcome the sense of separateness and to open our hearts to Loving Awareness of the All Being we are part of.

Studying the Torah can be of great help on our path to realization. After all, what is Torah? It is life transformed into sacred text! It is sacred not because it was transmitted to us by an external Divinity, but because of the intention that went into writing it. Studying Torah is like studying our lives, and in treating it as sacred we treat our lives as sacred and begin to live that way.

I believe the teachings of the Torah, when combined with the practice of mindfulness, offer a direct path to liberation, and it is my hope to share this path with you.

The Fundamental Problem of Human Life

Jewish mysticism revolves around a central quandary—a problem that mystics consider so fundamental that for them its solution defines the very task of human life. The problem is the rift that was created between human beings (and all they have created) on the one side and the Divine on the other. Since everything is God and nothing but God, the fundamental issue can actually be understood as a rift within the divine unity itself. This rift came about with the development of speech and language in our species, which then led to an organization of our mental processes that gives primacy to conceptual thinking.

According to the kabbalists, this rupture is at the root of our suffering. It causes a sense of separateness and disconnectedness from the whole, leading to the feelings of loneliness and alienation that afflict so many of us. For them, the cause of the rift is clear: our own actions are responsible; we humans have brought this condition upon ourselves. Accordingly, the fundamental task of human life is to repair the rift within the Godhead and restore divine unity, thus relieving our own suffering in the process.

I believe the mystics were essentially right in their assessment, and this book poses an understanding of their approach that both explains the origin of the rift and offers a way to heal it. It is my belief that the rift is a result of misperceptions created by our conceptual thinking and reinforced by our cultural conditioning. In particular, the usual concept of "self" is one that creates a profound sense of isolation from other beings, leaving us feeling lost and hopeless. Humans begin their lives in symbiotic relationship with a mother and thus have a deeply ingrained bodily memory of being connected to something outside of their own physicality. We all have a yearning to experience life as part of a whole. Such yearning is normal and in a sense even necessary, as in the long run it helps us in forging connections with others. But in the short run, the yearning is a manifestation of the alienated "self," a reminder of the painful rift that separates us from the whole. As such, the yearning self often sets us into a reactive mode that—be it protective or defensive—results in self-serving and self-centered actions, which in turn create only more suffering.

It's a natural inclination for us to accumulate pleasant experiences and protect ourselves from unpleasant ones; after all, that's precisely what our "self" is designed to do. But the side effect of this tendency is a pervasive fear that others may deprive or hurt us, and this fear leads us to erect mental barriers to keep pain at bay. With every new defense we set up, however, we alienate ourselves a little further, ultimately fueling a sense of profound loneliness. What began as a misperception that others are separate (and often hostile) forces has spiraled into an ever-deepening sense of isolation.

I appreciate this teaching of human responsibility as the cause of the alienation we experience, because it places supreme significance on our actions (which include thought, speech, and deed) and the choices we make in our lives. It is this sense of causality that is at the heart of the Jewish mystics' belief that our primary task in life is to repair the rift in the Godhead and thus help all beings recognize their interconnectedness and unity. Since "connection" is another way of saying "love," we may also say that it is our job to allow Loving Attention to dispel the faulty perceptions created by our mind. Waking up to the truth of what is, moment by moment, is the sacred commission of life.

The Side Effects of Conceptual Thinking

Before we begin our exploration, I would like to clarify that I don't believe conceptual thinking and language are in and of themselves bad or harmful; in fact, they have allowed for the appreciation and creation of beauty and for great leaps in wisdom and understanding. Conceptual thinking and language are also manifestations of the Divine. But it is also crucial to recognize their limitations, or to be more precise, the limitations they impose on our perception of reality. This is like the warning label for side effects that we see attached to otherwise helpful products. Simply put, concepts are names that we attach to things—but they give the impression that the objects so named are static, more or less unchanging and separate from other objects. But the reality, which words are meant to capture, is dynamic and ever changing. Imagine a photo of the Mississippi River. If taken by a good photographer, it may capture the river's majesty, its serenity, the particular colors of that day, and so on. But even the best photo can give us only a snapshot of one particular scene at one particular moment. The river constantly changes; a day of flooding and that very same vista will be rendered unrecognizable.

Such is the nature of Being: ever changing, flowing, a current of interrelated things and events arising and passing. The problem with labeling this Flow of Being in static, discrete terms is that our perception itself is being limited by it; after all, words and concepts frame *what* we store in our consciousness and *how* we store it. Rather than seeing reality for what it is, we begin to see things as static, immutable, and separate from one another.

This impact of words is heightened when we switch from the spoken word to the written word. The rabbis who shaped the practice of Rabbinic Judaism (in the first two centuries of the Common Era) argued about the benefits versus the dangers of fixating and codifying their oral tradition, which had begun over a thousand years earlier and was directly attributed to Moses and God. While some championed writing the teachings down to ensure they were not lost, many believed that the written word, even more static than the spoken, was thus further removed from the dynamic primal reality.

We find a slightly more contemporary version of this same tension in a tale of the Baal Shem Tov. The Besht regularly engaged with his students to help them practice ways to experience the Divine Presence in each moment. One night, he had a dream in which his adversary *hasatan* appeared to him. His adversary was dancing around the Besht in glee, holding up a book, teasing him, "Now I can defeat you. Now that I have a book of your teachings, I can defeat you." The Besht woke up from the dream and was greatly concerned. It was not his custom to write down any of his teachings, and his students were not supposed to write them down either. So he went to the house of study that day and confronted his students, "Has any among you been writing down what I have been saying?" One student sheepishly admitted to having recorded his words (meticulously, we may assume, and as verbatim as can be expected from a bright student with a good memory). The Besht demanded to see what the student had been writing, and, looking over his notes, he exclaimed, "Not one word in here is my teaching!"

I think there is great depth and wisdom in this story. The Besht dedicated his life's work to helping his students achieve a connection with the Divine through spiritual practice and direct experience. He taught more by the evidence of his being than his words. When he and his students were together, they experienced the Divine through their shared encounter. In a way, the words that were spoken (those recorded by the student) were extraneous to that experience and were indeed not his teaching. Whenever someone's living experience is condensed into written words, these words can be misconstrued and denigrated. That's what his adversary was gloating over.

Reconceptionism: A New Spiritual Methodology

One way to break the firm grip language holds over us is a method I call reconceptionism. By "reconceptionism" I mean a system for examining the nature of language and its impact on us. This method goes beyond intellectual analysis; when we reconceptualize, we actually change our relationship to concepts, beliefs, and opinions. The basic principle here is far from being new; historically, almost every Jewish approach to sacred texts has included a component of unearthing deeper truths by reinterpreting or even changing the literal meaning of a text. But reconceptionism does not (or at least not primarily) seek to replace an older, faulty concept with a newer, better, deeper one. It is by its nature an experiential approach, a practice for cultivating mindfulness of words and thoughts. It fosters an awareness of how concepts impact our consciousness and can help prevent us from reifying (or even idolizing) concepts by rendering transparent the limitations of our linguistic grasp of reality. In that sense, reconceptualizing is part of awakening from the linguistic matrix that holds us captive in ignorance.

I will in particular point out two interrelated techniques. The first has been developed and used extensively by the kabbalists. Their texts and teachings are notoriously difficult to penetrate; it's as if they were written in a different language, in Kabbalese, because they often reflect experiences of an altered consciousness, and it is difficult to understand these teachings without entering that consciousness. But there is a great deal of wisdom in the kabbalists' techniques. Our Jewish mystical ancestors had a deep commitment to the words of the inherited Jewish tradition, including all the sacred canonical texts, the Torah, the Prophets, and the collections of books referred to as the Writings (e.g., Psalms, Proverbs, Song of Songs). But following the longstanding Jewish methodology I alluded to earlier, the kabbalists felt free to explore those texts for their secret meanings by deconstructing words and even grammar and then reusing the raw material as building blocks for the construction of new worlds. This is essentially an analytical methodology, but one with new ground rules that break the hold of conventional understanding of the meaning of words and sentences. My hope is that this method will become clearer as I relay examples later in this book.

The other technique also relies on letting go of our old notions of reality in order to create new ones, but this one is derived from mystical spiritual experiences that promote altered consciousness. This method is rooted in various Jewish meditation practices. It is my sense that these practices are what led Jewish mystics to the insights that they later applied in reanalyzing the meaning of our sacred texts.

In our generation, this experiential Jewish meditative approach has taken on the form of Jewish mindfulness meditation and involves cultivating mindful, Loving Attention to the truth of each moment, here and now. Mindful, Loving Attention is awakened, clear, balanced, nonjudgmental, appreciative attention to the present moment of experience. In Jewish meditation as I practice it, the present moment of experience is equivalent to the Divine manifesting as the Present Moment of Being. The possibility of being awake and fully present in the moment is itself an instance of Divine Awareness. In addition, everything that is experienced from the "awake" position is also a manifestation of Being. When we observe our experiences through this lens, it is possible to begin to heal and to close the rift. Vital to this kind of awareness is an acceptance of knowing all aspects of the experience, not rejecting or filtering out anything unwanted. To fully accept and embrace whatever occurs as the truth of this moment is an act of love, and when our awareness is nurtured by Loving Attention, we gain true insight and wisdom from this attention. It allows the defenses around our hearts to soften and ultimately leads us to compassion and kindness toward others and also ourselves. At the end of part II, I will introduce an exercise to practice this kind of awareness.

Now, let's start our exploration by looking into one of the oldest testimonies of the arising of human consciousness, the Torah.

Part I

The Dualistic Misperception of Reality

1

The Torah and the Arising of Human Consciousness

B'reshit bara Elohim, the Torah opens.[1] The translation most of us are familiar with reads, "In the beginning, God created ..." Much has been written about this opening line, and when I first started to study the Torah, I understood this as the Jewish story about the creation of the earth. Many decades later, however, I've come to believe that this is not the case. My own interpretation is one that I've developed over the years, partially based on what I have learned from my teachers, but primarily out of my own reflections around the age-old question "What is this life that I have been given?" The opening stories of the Torah, I believe, speak to this question. They are indeed a creation story, but not about the beginning of earth. Rather, I believe that these opening stories capture in words, images, and metaphors the arising or birth or creation of human consciousness.

I believe the stories of the Torah were created by people who were examining questions similar to the ones you and I are interested in now. The books of Genesis and Exodus especially address the inquiries: Who are we? Why is life unfolding the way it is? Where does all this suffering come from, and is there a way out of the mess? What is the role of God in all this? Instead of forming theoretical explanations, our ancestors initially created stories to pass on their insights and wisdom. I believe they had some intuitive understanding of the vast process that allowed human beings to come into being. Stories were a perfect vehicle for this kind of intuitive understanding, and over time their collective artistry and wisdom produced a flowing narrative with chapter divisions that inadvertently highlight key events in the emergence of human consciousness.

In a Beginning

Let's start at the very beginning of their stories.

The Torah's first letter is the Hebrew letter *bet*. *Bet* is the second letter of the Hebrew alphabet (*aleph* being the first), and many generations of Jewish thinkers have wondered why the Torah begins with the second letter of the alphabet (or *aleph-bet*); after all, why not start the story of the beginning of creation with the first letter?

The Hebrew alphabet has always been used as a numerical system for counting as well as for creating words. The first nine letters of the alphabet correspond to the digits 1–9; so *aleph* represents the number 1, and *bet* represents the number 2. Perhaps, some thinkers speculated, by beginning with the letter *bet*, the Torah is telling us that this is not the first story, the *aleph* story, of creation. There are many stories about creation; in fact, the second chapter of Genesis also offers a creation story, one that is different from the one in the first chapter. Hence, the introduction requires a very careful investigation.

When we look at the first three words of the Torah, we notice that there is something wrong with the standard translation. First, we have to keep in mind that the Torah was written down using only consonants; vowels were not part of the written Torah (a standard practice that is used in most Hebrew texts to this day). The vowel sounds were understood simply by the context of the written word. This omission creates a certain ambiguity, as it opens the text to questions of pronunciation, which in turn have a large impact on the meaning of the words. While the standard Torah text has a now commonly accepted vocalization pattern, this pattern was not established until the tenth century CE. *B'reshit* (the accepted vocalization of the first word) is usually translated as "In the beginning"; this, however, is significantly inaccurate. **Bah**-*reshit* would be the Hebrew vocalization if the intended meaning was "In the beginning." The vocalization **b'***reshit* of the opening word, however, clearly leaves out the definite article. The accurate translation should read "In *a* beginning ..." instead. What a difference between these two versions!

"A beginning" immediately and intentionally leaves open the issue of which beginning, or the beginning of what; it is more akin to an opening phrase like "once upon a time." This gives weight to the notion that the Hebrew letter *bet* might indeed be a clue that this is not the first creation story, but rather the story of the creation of a world characterized by a separation rather than a more primal experience of undivided oneness. This is the story of the creation of duality (*bet* = 2) rather than a description of *aleph* or oneness. We will find further support for this idea in the story of the exile from the Garden of Eden. (We'll talk about this in chapter 2.) For now, we have moved from "In *the* beginning God created ..." to "In *a* beginning God created...."

In addition to this, the opening line of the Torah, *B'reshit bara Elohim*, is open to yet another radical interpretation. Individually the words mean: *b'reshit*, "in a beginning"; *bara*, "created"; *Elohim*, "God." Now, the word "God," *Elohim*, is normally assumed to be the subject of the sentence, that is, "In a beginning, God created...." The usual biblical order puts the subject after the verb, and then the object follows that. However, this is not a hard and fast rule, and since the word *Elohim* actually appears following the verb "created," *bara*, it is possible to interpret the sentence as saying *Elohim* (God) is what was created. This very understanding is the one offered by the Zohar, the classical book of Jewish mysticism, published by Moses de Leon in the thirteenth century in Spain. The Zohar asks us to consider the actual order of the words in the Torah, which implies that *Elohim* was the object that was created, rather than the subject, that is, the creator: "In a beginning God was created." That should sound like a fairly radical statement. Or it should sound radical if you thought God was the creator in this story rather than the creation. I believe the Zohar opens us up to seeing it both ways, which is in itself an opening to seeing the Divine in a new way.

In the Jewish mystical terminology derived from the Zohar, there are various names for different aspects of the Divine. The one called *Elohim* is a reference to the divine quality that manifests as *Binah* (understanding). According to the Zohar, this divine aspect was created through the agency of another divine aspect: intuitive wisdom, signified by the Hebrew word *Hochmah*. My sense is that when our human ancestors composed this opening line of Torah, they were mirroring the way that human beings had used their intuitive wisdom when they initially began to create God concepts. They must have recognized, perhaps unconsciously, that both wisdom and understanding, human qualities, are manifestations of something beyond us, and they called the forces that brought them into being "Gods" (*Elohim*). Essentially, the creation of God concepts is an attempt to explain the source of intuitive wisdom.

The Zohar addresses the fundamental problem I described earlier. From its mystical perspective, the move from oneness to duality can be seen in the move from *Hochmah* to *Binah*. These are the first two divine manifestations in the system called the ten *sefirot* (emanations). The word *Binah* (understanding) is related to the Hebrew word *bayn*, which means "between." Understanding (*Binah*) recognizes the connections *between* things. In order for there to be connections between things there must be at least two things, hence the dualistic nature of *Binah*. It takes intuitive wisdom, which is the flash of insight associated with oneness and puts it into a context with other moments of insight. "Insight" refers to the preverbal "aha" moment. *Binah* then puts an insight into language that can be conveyed to another person. In linking the God name/concept *Elohim* to the quality of understanding, the Zohar fully recognizes the implications for this opening line of Torah. This is the story of the creation of dualistic perspective, or the One that becomes Two.

Why did our ancestors use *Elohim* as a God name thousands of years before the Zohar linked its meaning to the quality of understanding? *Elohim* is a plural noun form in Hebrew and refers back to the notion of multiple Gods, which was rather common at the time the Torah was composed and written down. The concept of monotheism had not yet arisen when our human (as opposed to Jewish) ancestors began telling the story of their origin. They intuited something beyond themselves, but this was still an early stage of development of the human mind. What led up to this story? In the following paragraphs, I will describe a scenario in which the beginning or "coming into being" of conceptual thought following the onset of speech and language gave rise to a great many concepts, including those of powers that control the flow of life, the concepts we think of as Gods.

So, in a beginning, human beings created God concepts. This stage had to be preceded by the origin of conceptual thinking. I will argue that the creation story told in Genesis is a story about the origin of human consciousness. This does not imply that there isn't something outside of human consciousness that we might refer to as God. But I do think it is true that we humans created (and continue to create) the concepts we are using to refer to the Divine and, furthermore, that these concepts color our understanding of everything we experience.

The Creation of Human Beings

The second and third chapters of Genesis give us the story of the expulsion from the Garden of Eden. The tale is often thought of as a description of humanity's fall from grace, and in its most simplified version it reads like this: God creates Adam, and God tells Adam, the first human, not to eat the fruit from a particular tree in the garden. Adam eats it anyway, and so God banishes this being from the garden. The plot is very simple: God commands Adam; Adam disobeys; God punishes Adam. All of this presupposes a God who first made the earth and then created Adam.

When viewing Genesis as the story of the origin of human consciousness, however, a radically different meaning emerges. Following the methodology of the kabbalists and some of their explicit teachings about the subject, I searched these chapters for a deeper truth about the human condition and our fundamental problem: alienation from ourselves, from each other, from the world, and from God. Human consciousness as I am describing it did not come into being at the same time as *Homo sapiens* did. Our species seems to have originated approximately two hundred thousand years ago, and it's fair to assume that the cognitive processes of our earliest ancestors were rather different from those that took place tens of thousands of years later. The story that's told in Genesis clearly stretches past the initial creation of the species and points to a development that occurred in stages over a significant period of time. In the beginning, Adam is earthlike (*adamah* is "earth" in Hebrew), somewhat unconscious, not yet divided into man and woman—only later becoming Adam and Eve, but holding the potential of becoming something more complex. This initial earth being, a member of *Homo sapiens*, only later becomes a human being, and it is precisely this development that is at the heart of the story.

When *Homo sapiens* first entered the scene, they did not, or at least not immediately, have language at their disposal. This is still true of babies of our species. Of course, there are rival theories about the origins of language, a discussion I won't enter into here. What I will claim though is that our earliest ancestors didn't initially use words and abstract concepts to communicate with each other; their perception of the outer and the inner universe was not yet structured by concepts. At some later point then, likely tens of thousands of years after the appearance of *Homo sapiens*, language as we know it came into being—as a slow, evolutionary process. This development of language distinguishes human beings from earlier *Homo sapiens* as I am defining the terms.

Many life forms are capable of thinking and processing data, but conceptual thinking is different. Concepts are constructions of the mind that are superimposed on reality, primarily to facilitate the ability to navigate our environment, avoid pitfalls, and find more pleasant outcomes. By their very nature, concepts separate reality into discrete packets. In order to have a "sky," there has to be something that is "not sky." To have a "me," there has to be "not me." Concepts, we can say, are in this sense binary by nature.

This binary nature of concepts fosters dualistic thinking, which in turn leads to the loss of a sense of connection to the whole. It divides up reality, creates differences and opposites, and thus starts the process of separation that then leads to alienation. This is what the Torah story of creation, starting with that second letter, *bet*, is about. We can say the Torah captures the onset of dualistic thinking that arose with language. It exposes the inevitable loss of unity, of oneness with the Holy One of Being through human beings' creation of Gods (or God concepts). We started worshiping the God concepts (as well as many other concepts) and continue to do so over and over, moment by moment. These concepts were devised and agreed upon through a collective process, yet ironically they are at the very root of what keeps us isolated and alone.

If indeed the Torah authors explored the same question we are pursuing here—"What is it about human life that causes separation?"—then to fully understand we must closely read the second and third chapters of Genesis.

The Origin of Good and Evil

The second creation story begins in the fourth verse of Genesis 2, following the first three verses, which are still part of the seven-day story of creation begun in chapter 1 and describe the seventh day. It is interesting that the six days "of creation" are part of chapter 1, but not the seventh; somehow it is not a day like the others (we'll return to that later).

> ⁴ These are the begettings of the heavens and the earth: their being created.
> At the time of YHVH, God's making of earth and heaven,
> ⁵ no bush of the field was yet on earth,
> no plant of the field had yet sprung up,
> for YHVH, God, had not made it rain upon earth,
> and there was no human/*adam* to till the soil/*adamah*—
> ⁶ but a surge would well up from the ground and water all the face of the soil;
> ⁷ and YHVH, God, formed [*va-yeetzer*] the human, of dust from the soil,
> He blew into [the human's] nostrils the breath of life [*nishmat chayyim*]
> and the human became a living being [*l'nefesh chayah*].
> GENESIS 2:4–7

In this book I will occasionally make reference to the appendix, where I have included some contemplative practices to go along with the material I am discussing. These practices are meant to give some spiritual and experiential access beyond the conceptual approach. At this point I call your attention to practice 1 in the appendix. In order to feel the immediacy of the idea of the breath of life, the reader is encouraged to try out this practice before continuing. In general, it is a good practice to use to strengthen the connection between the breath, human life, and the Divine. While much more will be said later in the book about using the letters *yud, hay, vav,* and *hay,* it can be helpful to develop a relationship to these letters as a metaphoric experience of a relationship with the Divine.

Returning to the text, Genesis 2:7, which is about the creation of humankind, contains a number of key terms that will later be used by Jewish mystics in their system of explaining the Divine. We see terms like *YHVH* (the divine name), *chayah* (life), *yetzirah* (formation), and *neshamah* and *nefesh* (both terms for the soul or spirit). In Genesis 2:4 we also have the first occurrence in the Torah of the tetragrammaton (the four-letter divine name), *YHVH*. It is paired with *Elohim* and appears in the above translation as "YHVH, God." In verse 7, this YHVH, God, formed human beings.

The word "formed" that is used in Genesis 2:7 is *va-yeetzer*, in the third person masculine. The word in Hebrew is written with two *yud*s when only one is needed. An extra letter in a word is something that each generation of students of the Torah pays careful attention to when explaining its deeper meanings. Traditionally, this particular word with its double *yud* was seen as an indication that human beings were created with a twofold nature, a good inclination (*yetzer ha-tov*) and a bad inclination (*yetzer ha-ra*). But I think we can interpret this in another way. I mentioned earlier the large time gap between the origin of humans and the origin of language; I believe that here we might see a hint of this gap. A *neshamah* (soul) of life (*nishmat chayyim*) was breathed into the earthling, but what came into being is only called a living *nefesh* (*nefesh chayah*). In other words, in its earliest developmental stage *Homo sapiens* were characterized by *nefesh* but had not yet realized the full potential of this *neshamah* that would later become characteristic of our species. The term *nefesh chayah* (living soul) was first used in Genesis 1:20, when the first "living creatures" (water swarms) came into being. All the living beings of Genesis 1 have *nefesh*. The concept of *neshamah* is first introduced here in 2:7.

Another way to look at it is through the lens of evolutionary biology. We know that the brains of mammals contain older structures such as the brain stem and the limbic brain and that over time a cortex formed on top of these. These older structures remain in place, however, and are still effective; we could call them our "reptilian brain." Perhaps it is the reptilian brain function that is referred to by the phrase *nefesh chayah* in Genesis 2:7—the way we humans functioned before the *neshamah* fully emerged.

> [8] YHVH, God, planted a garden in Eden / Land-of-Pleasure, in the east,
> and there He placed the human whom He had formed.
> [9] YHVH, God, caused to spring up from the soil
> every type of tree, desirable to look at and good to eat,
> and the Tree of Life in the midst of the garden
> and the Tree of the Knowing of Good and Evil....
> [15] YHVH, God, took the human and set [the human] in the Garden of
> Eden,
> to work it and to watch it.
> [16] YHVH, God, commanded concerning the human, saying:
> From every (other) tree of the garden you may eat, yes, eat
> [17] but from the Tree of the Knowing of Good and Evil—
> you are not to eat from it,
> for on the day that you eat from it, you must die, yes, die.
> GENESIS 2:8–9, 2:15–17

I believe our early storytelling ancestors wanted to explain here who we are and how we came to be in the predicament of living lives that, while often wonderful, are also painfully challenging. This is the sense we have of living in exile from the Garden of Eden, or paradise. Early humans, similarly to us, faced violence, tribal warfare, and a constant struggle to survive. Using language, they described their experience of a world filled with good and evil, and it's within that matrix that they sought to explain the origin of their difficulties. It is fascinating to see how the issue of good and evil is placed front and center as the first thing discussed following the creation of human beings. In their telling of the story of creation, everything about the creation was good until they came along. On the first day, light was created, and it was good; on the second day, the firmament was created, and it was good; on the third day, the earth and the seas were formed, as was plant life, and all that was good;

on the fourth day, the sun and moon were created and they were good; on the fifth day, birds and swimming creatures were called good; on the sixth day, land-based creatures were called good. And in the first iteration of the creation of earthlings, they too were good (Genesis 1:31).

Now we move from the first creation story to the second creation story—a direct reflection of the idea that there is more than one story about creation. And in keeping with the other explorations in this book, that is where we come into trouble. "Good" and "evil" enter as a dualistic pair following the second mention of the formation of earthlings—of Adam/Eve, who receives a living *neshamah* (Genesis 2:7). Initially Adam/Eve is placed in an idyllic situation—the Garden of Eden (2:8). Yet, somehow, contained in the idyllic world is a tree that opens the possibility of knowing good and evil (2:9). The story is about to turn to the origin of problems for our species.

Another important move from one to two follows soon after the introduction of good and evil. Initially there is only one being, Adam/Eve, not yet separated by gender. Not wanting Adam/Eve to be alone (Genesis 2:18), YHVH, God, goes on to create a second human by putting Adam/Eve to sleep, taking one of Adam/Eve's ribs (2:21), and from it forming a woman (2:22). This step obviously marks a crucial juncture in the development of human beings. Where there was only one human, now there are two. Rather than just beginning the story with the existence of males and females (an assumption that is made with the animals), a fissure is introduced, a split that I believe the Torah uses to introduce the concept of duality. Perhaps this suggests the split from a unified sense of humanity, Adam/Eve, into separate human beings, Adam and Eve. It is after that split that the problems begin.

These two beings are not yet fully conscious, at least not in the way we think of consciousness. They are the creatures of the garden that have not yet seen the world through the lens (conceptual framework) of good and evil. They are characterized as naked and unknowing, naive. Chapter 2 ends with the verse "Now the two of them, the human and his wife, were nude, yet they were not ashamed" (Genesis 2:25). They were in their infancy and innocent of good and evil; conscious but not "self" conscious.

The Fall of Humanity

What follows then is often referred to as "the fall," and creatures who remind us of ourselves come onto the scene. (Note: Ellipses appear in the translation itself.)

[1] Now the snake was more shrewd than all the living-things of the field that YHVH, God, had made.

It said to the woman:

Even though God said: You are not to eat from any of the trees in the garden…!

[2] The woman said to the snake:

From the fruit of the (other) trees in the garden we may eat,

[3] but from the fruit of the tree that is in the midst of the garden, God has said:

You are not to eat from it and you are not to touch it,

lest you die.

[4] The snake said to the woman:

Die, you will not die!

[5] Rather, God knows

that on the day that you eat from it, your eyes will be opened

and you will become like gods, knowing good and evil.

[6] The woman saw

that the tree was good for eating

and that it was a delight to the eyes,

and the tree was desirable to contemplate.

She took from its fruit and ate

and gave also to her husband beside her,

and he ate.

⁷ The eyes of the two of them were opened

and they knew then

that they were nude.

They sewed fig leaves together and made themselves loincloths.

⁸ Now they heard the sound of YHVH, God, (who was) walking about
in the garden at the breezy-time of the day.

And the human and his wife hid themselves from the face of YHVH,
God, amid the trees of the garden.

⁹ YHVH, God, called to the human and said to him:

Where are you?

¹⁰ He said:

I heard the sound of You in the garden and I was afraid, because I am
nude,

and so I hid myself.

¹¹ He said:

Who told you that you are nude?

From the tree about which I command you not to eat,

have you eaten?

¹² The human said:

The woman whom You gave to be beside me, she gave me from the
tree,

and so I ate.

¹³ YHVH, God, said to the woman:

What is this that you have done?

The woman said:

The snake enticed me,

and so I ate.

GENESIS 3:1–13

In the next few lines, God curses the snake (Genesis 3:14) and predicts that women and snakes in the future will be enemies (v. 15). God also states that the woman's deed will cause her to have pain at childbirth (v. 16). God tells the human that the soil will be damned for the human, causing the need for arduous labor in order to get food (v. 17). God also points out for the first time that the earthling will return to the earth (v. 19). (The temporality of human life is introduced for the first time here; it is unclear if it is part of the punishment or something that would have been the case anyway. In either case, it is not called death here but "returning," for the human was dust and returns to dust.)

> ¹⁹ By the sweat of your brow shall you eat bread,
>   until you return to the soil,
>   for from it you were taken.
>   For you are dust, and to dust shall you return.
> ²⁰ The human called his wife's name: Havva / Life-giver!
>   For she became the mother of all the living.
> ²¹ Now YHVH, God, made Adam and his wife coats of skins and clothed
>   them.
> ²² YHVH, God, said:
>   Here, the human has become like one of us, in knowing good and
>   evil.
>   So-now, lest he send forth his hand
>   and take also from the Tree of Life
>   and eat
>   and live throughout the ages…!
> ²³ So YHVH, God, sent him away from the Garden of Eden, to work
>   the soil from which he had been taken.
> ²⁴ He drove the human out
>   and caused to dwell, eastward of the Garden of Eden,
>   the winged-sphinxes and the flashing, ever-turning sword
>   to watch over the way to the Tree of Life.
>   GENESIS 3:19–24

On its face, this seems to be the tale of a creator God deliberately setting up God's creatures to fall. Why would God plant a tree and then tell a naive being not to eat from it? What would be the point unless God wanted just that to happen? In this version of the fall, an external God tempts God's own creation. I am not particularly moved by the story with that interpretation. It is a childish version of explaining difficulties through the laying of blame. God is blamed for making the Tree of the Knowing of Good and Evil in the first place. The snake is then blamed for telling the woman partner of Adam to eat from the tree. Adam blames the woman for giving him fruit of the tree. (The language of "him and her" fits in this instance because the separation of gender is a part of the blame game of the story at this point.) At every turn in the story, responsibility and blame are assigned. Now, why would human beings create such a story? Why are they looking to place the blame for their condition somewhere else? Because on one level, most of the time, that is exactly what we all do.

If you take a step back and look for a deeper meaning, however, the story becomes more interesting. Instead of seeing this as a historical account, I read it as an early attempt by human beings to project their internal pain onto external reality. Rather than understanding challenges and even evil as products of our human nature, they are assigned to an external factor, the snake. Rather than understanding pain and toil as our existential condition, they are explained as something imposed on us. Projection is a phase in the development of human consciousness that divides the world into self and other. But as human consciousness has further developed and matured, a more profound wisdom and understanding have become possible. We are able to look at the things we do, say, or think and ask probing questions about their causes and meanings.

For example, the word used for describing Adam and Eve as naked or nude is *arumim*, plural of *arum* (naked) (Genesis 2:25). Perhaps this means they were not "self" conscious yet; they were still naive or childlike. In the very next verse, the serpent is introduced with just the same word: *V'hanachash hayah arum* (Genesis 3:1). This is usually translated, "Now the snake was cunning." However, the use of the same adjective to describe the humans and the snake in successive sentences suggests a different reading, one that points to the similarity between them. The use of parallel language supports the notion that it was not some external voice telling the humans to eat the fruit; instead, the snake—that is, the reptilian brain—is part of our own nature.

Reflecting on how our ancestors used specific words in an attempt to understand their inner process is for me an important step. This kind of self-exploration points to a new use of consciousness by human beings. The first shift we saw was the introduction of conceptual thinking. In a beginning, Gods (*Elohim*) were created; that is, human beings—using language to reflect upon the world—came up with the concept of Gods. Now we can see how this capability has been (and is still) used: we project onto that concept the responsibility for having created the difficult world we live in.

Understanding our *own* responsibility in this is critical for our emancipation from this paradigm. We must see that we created and are continuing to create the world(s) we live in as well as the God concepts we blame for this creation. The origin of speech and language in *Homo sapiens* was such a stunning development that the brains of our species were essentially co-opted by discursive thinking. By and large, we do not live in the "natural" world; we live in worlds made up of beliefs and opinions about reality and how we want reality to look. Cultures and civilizations are defined by our shared beliefs, and those beliefs come into being through the power of language. The Torah says that God spoke the world into being. I used to think that this was a metaphor, but I now see that the worlds of virtual reality we inhabit most of the time are in fact spoken into being—not by an external God, but by us.

2

Speech in Exile

The Zohar's Reading of the Garden Story
and the Corruption of Language

The Jewish mystics held the belief that the world we live in was spoken into being by God through the vehicle of the Hebrew language. Their practices were founded on a spiritual lineage that saw God's word as the interface between God and the world of humans, and—as mentioned earlier—their key mystical techniques focused on deconstructing language, a process that for them opened up mystical experiences of alternate realities. My own approach starts from a different premise but often reaches similar conclusions. I don't think God created language separate and apart from its use by human beings and then used it to shape the world and everything in it (the main premise of the mystics). I do, however, believe that language is part of the divine Unfolding of Being and that it plays a key role in shaping the various worlds we live in, such as Western civilization, our cultures, and our subcultures. Because of this role, it is important to develop a contemplative practice that allows us to rest in awareness of the flow of language and its impact on our own heart/mind; it is this awareness that allows us to move beyond conditioned beliefs and open up to new insights on the nature of reality.

My own position is hence close enough to the mystics' beliefs and experiences that I consider myself in their lineage, yet different enough to come to different conclusions.

As I searched their teachings for the insights about life that the kabbalists imputed to the same passages of Torah discussed above, I found a reading in the Zohar of the expulsion from paradise story that raises an extraordinary assertion: that we do not know "who drove out whom." Here is the passage in question:

> [23] So YHVH, God, sent him away from the Garden of Eden, to work the soil from which he had been taken.
> [24] He drove the human out.
>
> GENESIS 3:23–24

Most commentators immediately notice a problem here: redundancy. In Genesis 3:23, Adam is sent away from the garden, and then verse 24 says "he drove the human out." Why restate in verse 24 what has just been said in verse 23; why the repetition? The Zohar's response is that these two verses don't contain a repetition at all; in fact, what they see here is a hidden teaching not only of profound depth but also of extraordinary importance to our focus in this book.

Before we delve into the Zohar's approach, it's worthwhile reminding ourselves that the Zohar can be rather difficult to understand. (To many of us, the Zohar passage below reads a bit like Abbott and Costello's skit "Who's on First?") Fortunately, we have a contemporary scholar, Daniel Matt, whose annotated translation of the Zohar makes it much more accessible. In the following, I will draw on Daniel Matt's commentary.

Genesis 3:24 begins with the three Hebrew words *va-y'garesh et ha-adam*. *Va-y'garesh* can mean to "drive away," but it is also closely related to the Hebrew word for "divorce," *gerushin*. The authors of the Zohar use this latter meaning, suggesting that the verse indicates a divorce that occurred as a result of what had transpired. The question then is, who divorced whom? Did God divorce humanity because of humanity's sin, or did humanity cause some other kind of divorce? Virtually all explanations before the Zohar believed that God drove out the human because of humanity's bad behavior. By contrast, the Zohar sees this event as a divorce, a divorce that—incredibly—occurs entirely within the Godhead. One part of God gets divorced from another part of God, and according to the Zohar, humanity (Adam) is to be blamed for causing this divorce. The Zohar understands the Divine as manifesting in a tenfold set of emanations. The sixth emanation is called *Tiferet*, which is best understood as Divine Compassion, and is equated with the Tree of Life in the Garden of Eden. The Tree of the Knowing of Good and Evil is equated with the tenth emanation (*Shechinah* or *Malchut*, Kingdom). The divorce that the kabbalists see is a divorce within the Godhead, symbolized by separation or divorce of *Shechinah* from *Tiferet*.

In order to fully assert that it was Adam who caused this separation, they needed to deconstruct normal Hebrew grammar. In the phrase *va-y'garesh et ha-adam*, by normal rules of grammar, the Hebrew word *et* has no independent meaning; it is a grammatical construction that simply indicates that what follows is the direct object of the sentence. Hence, by standard rules, the human (*ha-adam*) is the direct object of this sentence, not the subject; thus, "He drove the human out" (Genesis 3:24).

The Zohar turns this relation upside down, claiming the opposite: that the human is the subject, and that it is the human who caused *et* to be divorced from God. Not only has the subject of the sentence changed here, but the word *et* has been given an altogether new meaning, becoming a noun. (This is exactly the kind of radical deconstruction of language that the kabbalists use to move past the normal meaning of words and uncover what they claim is the secret truth of the Torah.) It was Adam who caused a rift or divorce in the Godhead—more precisely, a rift in which a part of God, signified by *et*, was separated from the rest of God. Rabbi Shimon, the alleged author of the Zohar and one of its main characters, discusses the verses that describe the consequences of Adam's "sin" in eating from the Tree of the Knowing of Good and Evil:

> "YHVH Elohim expelled him from the Garden of Eden …
> He drove out *et* Adam" (Genesis 3:23–24).
> Rabbi Elazar said,
> "We do not know who drove out whom,
> if the Blessed Holy One divorced Adam
> or not.
> But the word is transposed:
> 'He drove out *et*.'
> *Et*, precisely!
> And who drove out *Et*?
> 'Adam,'
> Adam drove out *Et*!
> Therefore it is written:
> '*YHVH Elohim* expelled him from the Garden of Eden.'
> Why did He expel him?
> Because Adam drove out *Et*,
> as we have said."[1]

But what exactly is *et* to the authors of the Zohar? The Zohar asserts that *et* is a secret Torah code for the *Shechinah*, which is usually understood to be the feminine aspect of the Divine. It is likely that this feminine identification for *et* is drawn from the fact that these same two letters, *aleph* and *tav*, when pronounced with a different vowel, make up the word *at* (versus *et*), which is the Hebrew word for "you" in the feminine form. (The masculine form for "you" is *atah*.) The Zohar is asserting that the *Shechinah*, which one might say is this world we live in, comes about through the agency of language. *Aleph* and *tav*, the first and the last letters of the Hebrew alphabet and by inference all the rest of the letters between them, together make up the two-letter word/symbol *et*, and to the kabbalists *et* can hence be equated with the totality of everything God has spoken, reflecting their belief that our world was spoken into being by God.[2] According to the Zohar, the man caused *et* to become divorced from the rest of the Divine, specifically that part of the Divine signified by the Tree of Life, or *Tiferet*. If we follow this meaning, then it's the feminine aspect of the Divine that was split off from the masculine aspect. Daniel Matt's footnote reads:

> ***Et*, precisely!** In the Zohar *et* is a kabbalistic code name for *Shekhinah*, the last *sefirah*. Expressing the fullness of divine speech, *Shekhinah* spells out all the letters of the Hebrew alphabet, *alef* to *tav: et.*... Once *Et* was driven out of the Garden, language became corrupt and remained so until the Revelation at Sinai....
>
> **Adam drove out *Et*!** The nature of Adam's sin is one of the most tightly guarded secrets of the Zohar. The language of Genesis 3, the Garden story, is understood as hiding the true meaning of the sin; see *Zohar Hadash, Bereshit,* 19a (*Midrash ha-Ne'elam*), where Rabbi Shim'on recounts a conversation he had with Adam while selecting his future place in Paradise: "Adam ... was sitting next to me and speaking with me, and he asked that his sin not be revealed to the whole world beyond what the Torah had said concerning it. It is concealed in that tree in the Garden of Eden." The Tree of Knowledge of Good and Evil is a symbol of *Shekhinah*. Adam's sin was that he worshiped and partook of *Shekhinah* alone, thus splitting Her off from the higher *sefirot* and divorcing Her from Her husband, *Tif'eret*, the Tree of Life. Adam disrupted the unity of the cosmos and "severed the young trees" (*qitzetz ba-neti'ot*). This last image, employed by the Talmud to describe heresy, is applied by the Kabbalah to Adam's sin.... On the psychological plane, the sin corresponds to the splitting off of consciousness from the unconscious....
>
> Here, by means of a midrashic twist, Rabbi El'azar indicates that Adam has divorced *Shekhinah*. This may mean "divorced Her from *Tif'eret*" or "divorced Her from himself." The first

interpretation accords with the kabbalistic scheme outlined above; cf. Zohar 153a: "He caused a defect, separating the Wife from Her Husband."[3]

So, at this point in our argument we have two main assertions. First, Adam set in motion the divorce when he ate from a tree; and second, the tree was connected to speech. According to the Zohar, Adam's deed, by denying all aspects of the Divine except for *Shechinah*, was in essence an act of heresy (as heresy is understood as a distortion of the real truth of the totality of what God is).

This interpretation is very close to my own. In my mind, Adam represents all of us, humanity. We as a species created language; we created labels and concepts to describe the world around us and inside us and, by extension, our reality maps of the world we live in. However, we remained largely unaware of this process and its workings, and so we started (mis)taking our concepts for the reality itself and after a while began worshiping them (in particular, the concepts of God and of self). This process created a distortion (the objectification that comes with conceptualizing reality) and pro-duced a rift between the true nature of things and our concepts of them. As Daniel Matt references, Adam's sin "was that he wor-shiped and partook of *Shekhinah* alone, thus splitting Her off from the higher *sefirot* and divorcing Her from Her husband, *Tif'eret*, the Tree of Life."

This rift is at the heart of the classical teachings of Jewish mystics. They believe the world we live in is cut off from the so-called higher realms of the Divine. The *Shechinah*, the immanent aspect of the Divine, has gone into exile in this world. In psychological terms we would say that we are cut off from certain parts of ourselves, espe-cially our hearts. The same goes for the largely unconscious forces of lust and aversion. While these are natural phenomena of the rep-tilian and limbic systems, we often project them as an evil force or some other external entity and then fall victim to believing our own story, thus distorting the truth and creating separate realms of reality. In chapter 5, I'll return to this theme and explore in particular how we become addicted to our notion of a separate "self" and other attachments of our cultural conditioning.

In the story of the Garden of Eden there are two different trees, the Tree of Life, symbol of *Tiferet*, and the Tree of the Knowing of Good and Evil, symbol of the *Shechinah*. These trees are part of a system of ten emanations, or *sefirot* (plural), all of which are aspects of the divine oneness, of the single Unfolding of Being. *Tiferet* is often translated as "beauty"; in the context of our given discussion, however, it is more apt to emphasize this *sefirah*'s connection with the quality of compassion and the heart.

The system of these ten *sefirot* is visually arranged in three pillars, with the middle pillar being the pillar of balance. *Tiferet* is not only on that pillar, but it forms the center of the vertical arrangement. This is important because the arrangement of the *sefirot* is often superimposed on the form of a human body, and in that way *Tiferet*'s position connects it to the heart.

So, in making the claim that Adam's sin caused a divorce between husband *Tiferet* and wife *Shechinah*, the kabbalists are also saying that the world in which we are in exile with the *Shechinah* is cut off from the heart. I think this is a very astute interpretation in that it points to one of the negative side effects the use of language has inflicted on us: in breaking down the world into dualistic categories, language leaves us feeling cut off, separate, and lonely. The worlds we have created through the conceptual thinking process, which we usually experience as happening in our heads, separate us from our hearts and sever us from unity with others. As Daniel Matt points out, according to the kabbalists, "Once *Et* was driven out of the Garden, language became corrupt and remained so until the Revelation at Sinai." Or, as I would restate this, the corrupting nature of thinking is what drove us away from a sense of peace and ease and connection to life. What happened later at Mount Sinai then opened the door to reversing the process.

Into Exile

In its analysis of language's divisive role in the human condition, the Zohar goes a step further when it asserts another divorce, a divorce between speech and voice. For example, in the following verses from Exodus, Moses is instructed by God to go to the Pharaoh and tell him that he should let the children of Israel leave Egypt.

> [10] YHVH spoke to Moshe, saying:
> [11] Go in, speak to Pharaoh king of Egypt,
>   that he may send free the Children of Israel from his land.
> [12] Moshe spoke before YHVH, saying:
>   Here, (if) the Children of Israel do not hearken to me,
>   how will Pharaoh hearken to me?
>   —and I am of foreskinned lips.
>   EXODUS 6:10–12

The Zohar explains uncircumcised lips as a reference to the fact that since the time of the exile from the garden, speech is in exile from voice:

> Come and see: As long as speech was in exile, voice withdrew from it.... Moses was voice without word, which was in exile.... And so it continued until they approached Mount Sinai ... whereupon voice united with speech.[4]
>   ZOHAR ON VA-ERA 2:25B

What does this mean? How are speech and voice different? And how can one be "in exile" from the other? Here is the Zohar's bold claim, with running comments from Moshe Miller in brackets:

> However, this is the secret: Moses [was granted] voice [when God told him, "I will be with your mouth"], but speech as expression in words [referring to *malchut*] was [still] in exile. He was unable to express [himself in] words. And for this reason he said, "How will Pharaoh listen to me? As long as words are in exile, I have

26

no way to express myself. I [am on the level of] voice, but I am missing words, which are in exile." So the Holy Blessed One God partnered him with Aaron.

[The verse later states, "He shall speak for you to the people" (ibid. 4:16). Aaron was a prophet, and he was able to make the Divine presence—the *Shechinah*—manifest. By joining forces with Moses they would be able to make divine speech manifest to the Children of Israel. (Based on the *Ramaz*)]

Come and see: Throughout the time that speech was in exile, voice was disconnected from it, and speech was sealed up without a voice. But when Moses came [on the scene] voice arrived. But Moses was voice without speech, for speech was in exile. And as long as speech was in exile, Moses went as voice without speech [until he partnered with Aaron. But as far as Moses himself]—this situation continued until they came to Mount Sinai, when the Torah was given. At that time voice became joined with speech, and speech was expressed in words. And so it is written, "And God spoke all of these words, saying ..." (Exodus 20:1).[5]

Voice (*kol*) is clearly conceived as being distinct from speech here; the question is how. Speech, I believe, simply refers to the act of expressing oneself through words. To understand "voice," however, we have to take a step back. Let's look closely at what happened right after Adam ate from the tree (Genesis 3:6), as it was then and there, at the exact moment when knowledge of good and bad (duality) arose, that voice and speech were severed.

The Torah says, "The eyes of the two of them were opened and they knew then that they were nude" (Genesis 3:7). I think what we see here is a description of the moment humanity becomes *self-conscious*. Or put differently, what we see here is a story about the arising of the concept of a self: we humans are becoming conscious of having a (naked) self. The English expression "self-conscious" also has a connotation we are all familiar with: the judging and evaluating of our own worth. When we become self-conscious, we worry about whether our "self" is adequate to the task of getting what we need. Fear and doubt seep in, and to protect ourselves from being hurt (both physically and emotionally), we move into a defensive thinking mode. This is precisely what happens to the humans in the garden when they realize they are naked.

> [8] Now they heard the sound [or voice, *kol*] of YHVH, God, (who was) walking about in the garden at the breezy [*ruach*] time of the day.
>
> And the human and his wife hid themselves from the face of YHVH, God, amid the trees of the garden.
>
> [9] YHVH, God, called to the human and said to him:
>
> Where are you?
>
> [10] He said:
>
> I heard the sound [*kol*] of You in the garden and I was afraid, because I am nude,
>
> and so I hid myself.
>
> GENESIS 3:8–10

In these verses the humans are both defensive and also have become separate from the Divine, projecting the voice of God outside themselves. It is not entirely clear what it means to hear a voice (*kol*) walking, but in trying to decipher the spiritual message here, the Zohar sees a link in the verse between the *kol* walking and the word *ruach*, which for kabbalists is the spirit name for one of the four worlds of Being Unfolding. (In chapter 4, we will look at the four worlds.) For them, *ruach* (one of the four "worlds" of Being) is associated with the letter *vav*, which in Hebrew signifies "connecting." This will be explained as the world where Being manifests as "Loving." The quality called voice is an aspect of *ruach*, and the heart is the seat of that loving experience. Speech, on the other hand, is associated with conceptual thinking and the confusion and doubt that can be part of thinking with the head. Speech, we can say, is our head in exile from our heart.

I think this is a deep truth. Adam hid in the concept of "I am naked" and thoughts of guilt, because Adam was afraid of Adam's own heartfelt feelings of separation. The feelings of the heart are often very tender and sometimes painful, so we hide behind words ("I'm naked / guilty / bad"). When that happens, when we go to the defenses of the thinking mind and hide from our feelings, the heart then cries out to us, "Where are you?" as in Genesis 3:9.

This event marks a radical turning point in the story. Up until this point, the universe of Being Unfolding has been described throughout the story as "good." The six "days" of things coming into being were all described in chapter one as the "good" things. Then the seventh is a different kind of day, one that has its own chapter; it is no longer a day where good things come into being, but instead it is blessed and hallowed. So, what happened to the "good" universe of Being following the eating from the Tree of the Knowing of Good and Evil? What does it mean to live with a reality map that shows the world as good *and* bad? I think our dualistic reality map is what is meant by "Adam partook of *Shekhinah* alone."

In the story that immediately follows the expulsion, the Torah describes the effect of being in exile with this worldview. In Genesis 4, Adam and Eve give birth to two children, Cain and Abel. This next story is following up on the introduction of a dualistic perspective by immediately turning to a story of two children. As with many (perhaps most) children in a family, sibling rivalry and jealousy arise, but this time the result is extreme. Cain kills Abel. We eat from the Tree of the Knowing of Good and Evil, and the next story is about murder. So, once the exile caused by dualistic thinking is set into motion, things go quickly from good to evil, and the rest of the book of Genesis is a continuing saga of the descent into ever-deeper evil. It is basically all downhill from there. Life as a whole, for the protagonists of the story, the Hebrew people, gets more and more desperate until they all end up in exile in Egypt—*Mitzrayim*. (The Hebrew word *mitzrayim* has the root *tzor*, meaning "shut in" or "narrowness"; in the doublet form of Hebrew grammar, this word implies a doubly narrow place, a very tight squeeze.) At the start of Exodus, the next book of the Torah, we find that the Hebrew people have become slaves—the final outcome of a process that started with the fall. This then is the metaphoric story of just how bad things can get and have gotten for us human beings when we lose sight of the interconnectedness of all of Being Unfolding and begin to the see the world through the lens of good and evil.

As the downward slide of human history unfolds, there are still individual journeys that point us to what we need to do to turn things around. We will look, for example, at the story of Avram, the father of the Hebrew people, as a metaphor that can guide us in our individual practice. But it is only in Exodus that we will find the deep insight that can restore the world to holiness.

Looking ahead to the events at Sinai, we notice that the Divine is addressed as *YHVH*. This appellation for the Divine did not appear in the first chapter of Genesis, where *Elohim* was used for God. I believe this difference reflects when various storylines were added to the Torah: earlier, pre-Sinai stories use *Elohim*; later, post-Sinai stories use *YHVH*, before it was all canonized around 400 BCE. The *YHVH* tradition in Judaism has affected the way that the stories of Torah were told—even those that chronologically happen before Sinai. Therefore, I think it will be helpful to explore this tradition of referring to the Divine as *YHVH* now, and then return to Genesis and the events at Sinai.

Part II

Universalism and Particularism in the Jewish Mystics' Understanding of the Divine

3

What Is YHVH?

This book has been exploring the sense of separation that pervades human life. Internally, this separation is experienced as alienation from our own experience. Externally, it's experienced as a gap between our selves and everything that is perceived as "not self"; this can include what we call the world and what we call the Divine or God. The sense of separation isn't inevitable, however, and I invite you to contemplate a different way of relating to everything that is. This different way could be called "the mystic's path."

Jewish mystics need to reconcile two different, seemingly exclusive viewpoints, as do all mystics. On the one hand, there is mundane consciousness, which sees the world as composed of many individual things. On the other hand, there is the mystics' view that everything is actually part of a singularity; everything is one. Jewish mystics tackle the dilemma with a methodology that is particular to their linguistic approach. Their starting point is with the Hebrew letters *Yud Hay Vav Hay*, commonly assumed to be God's name. Rather than seeing the letters as merely a name, however, the mystics use them to deduce a theory that recognizes the relative reality of disparate objects and events and reconciles them with the absolute truth of oneness.

Let's start by looking at the poetic teaching of one of the Hasidic masters:

> What is the world? The world is God, wrapped in robes of God so as to appear to be material. And who are we? We are God wrapped in robes of God and our task is to unwrap the robes and thus dis-cover that we and all the world are God.[1]

This teaching is from Menahem Nahum of Chernobyl, a student of the Baal Shem Tov. I learned these words a few years after the core teaching of the Besht that I mentioned in the introduction, "Everything is God and nothing but God." Whether you are new to either of these teachings or not, take a moment to reflect on the significance of both. Give yourself a few minutes! What do these teachings evoke in you? Are you drawn to them? Does the God language turn you off? Perhaps you think, "I wish I could believe this"; or you wonder, "How can I have this experience?" Just investigate how the teachings resonate with you.

For me, both teachings are of tremendous importance. Not only are they at the core of my personal practice, but they also inform the general exploration of what I am presenting in this book. If nothing else, I hope they will inspire you to reflect on your own conceptualizations of God. After all, when we contemplate the nature of the Divine, we should keep in mind that "God" is only a word. My colleague and friend Norman Fischer likes to say, "I know what God is. God is a three-letter word found in an English dictionary." Rather than getting transfixed by a rigid notion of the word "God," we want to take the mystics' approach and directly investigate the manifestation of the Divine in the experience of life. It is from this direct experience that we can then try to conceptualize the experience in a way that fosters a sense of unity rather than causing a sense of separation.

"Everything is God and nothing but God" is such a helpful framework. It is such a *broad*-reaching concept that it can hold within it all other concepts of reality. As such, it serves the Jewish mystics' goal of explaining all of reality as contained within the Divine. But as helpful a concept as this is, the mystics wanted more than just an intellectual explanation; they wanted also an experiential appreciation of the divine nature of all life. Mystical realization goes beyond the theoretical, and in order to realize oneness we need to experience ourselves, our "selves," as part of the whole. I think that's precisely what the poetic rendering of Menahem Nahum aims at. In fact, he points us to four different aspects of the world. Let's take another look.

> What is the world? The world is God, wrapped in robes of God so as to appear to be material. And who are we? We are God wrapped in robes of God and our task is to unwrap the robes and thus dis-cover that we and all the world are God.

Menahem Nahum is saying that we and the world and the robes are all God. But there must be something about the nature of being human that causes this reality to be less than apparent. That's why he asks: "What is the world?" "Who are we?" He is affirming that there is a world, but the world's true nature is hidden in the robes that are wrapping it. One aspect of the world, I believe, can be seen as the material nature of reality, and the robes are some aspect that distorts our perception of the world; even the distortion, he claims, is itself also God. The robes or distortions are essentially our beliefs, views, and opinions about the world. What we think of as our selves are essentially nothing other than this same world. All of this is one aspect of a fourfold metaphor for the great oneness of the Divine—its corporeal nature.

Menahem Nahum then tells us that we have a function to perform: "Our task is to unwrap the robes." What he refers to is the "God-Process," relating to God more like a verb than a noun. We could say God-ing. Unwrapping the robes is the divine activity that we as divine beings are meant to participate in. The way we "unwrap the robes" is through paying Loving Attention, which I am equating with an aspect of divine manifestation, to the world and to its garments. By careful observation we see all the layers or garments that act as filters on our perceptions. This God-Process, Loving Attention, is the second aspect of a fourfold metaphor for the great oneness of the Divine.

We wouldn't be able to "discover" the world if it weren't for the fact that it is discoverable. The intuitive wisdom function of reality is different from its physical nature. From it arises the capacity for understanding the truth of things, and this is the third aspect Menahem Nahum is pointing us toward. He asserts that the true nature of the world can be beheld through the wisdom and clarity that come following Loving Attention. And this is itself the third aspect of God that is pointed toward in this teaching.

Finally, there is an implied fourth divine aspect, which I choose to call "awareness." As the world is beheld through Loving Attention, the nature of the world is known in awareness. As Loving Attention manifests, its functioning is also knowable in awareness. The insights that arise (in this case that we and the world are God) are also known in awareness. Awareness is that realm within which things can be known.

Taken together, this four-part approach is what the Jewish mystics call the four worlds model of the Divine. When I first learned about this model, it was typical to identify the four aspects with "Acting/Making/Doing," "Feeling," "Knowing," and "Being"; these words were commonly understood to summarize the realms. While I appreciate the simplicity of these four words, my experience has led me to expand on the nature of the four worlds in a more nuanced way. By "experience" I mean not only studying the model, but also applying it in my contemplative practice. My personal experience has led me to understand that paying Loving Attention to the world is a direct path to the realization of God loving God. It is part of the God-ing process.

It is no coincidence that our model comprises four worlds; after all, it originates with the mystical understanding of the four letters *Yud Hay Vav Hay* in the Jewish tradition. Jewish mystics have been generally committed to working within the boundaries of the language of sacred texts. Since the original injunction that this combination of letters be remembered throughout the generations, they have been commonly thought of as a name, the most holy name for God. This is true traditionally, as well as through the way most people understand the language and the story line of the Torah. Until today, most of the Jewish world still sees it that way. But as I have pointed out, this is a limiting view, and mystics have long sought a rather different approach. They have been generally preoccupied with the language of sacred texts. They interpret the four individual letters of the YHVH "name" as symbols of different worlds, parallel aspects of being. And since there were four letters, they created a model that comprised four overlapping yet distinct worlds.

Historically, Judaism operates under an injunction prohibiting the speaking aloud of this four-letter "name." It is unclear just exactly when the prohibition on pronouncing these letters as God's name arose, but by Talmudic times it was well established. YHVH became known as the ineffable or unutterable name. Since Hebrew is a language consisting only of consonants in its written form, the only way one could know the proper vocalization of that name was to learn it from another who already knew it. It seems possible that for some period its verbal usage became restricted to the priesthood and was kept secret within that priesthood. With the destruction of the Temple in 70 CE and the end of priestly function in that Temple, the oral tradition of correct pronunciation was lost. Many contemporary Jews believe that this refraining from speaking God's name is a beautiful way of pointing out the problem of how any name, in its finiteness, could be used to represent the infinite.

4

The Four Worlds Model

The mystics weren't satisfied with merely refraining from using YHVH as a name. They didn't think it solved the underlying problem of the infinite having a finite name. So, rather than merely seeing YHVH as a name, they suggested that the letters stood for four different yet overlapping "worlds" in which God "Gods" differently. From this, they developed a rich and complex theology that captures the way in which multiplicity and oneness can be held together. It sees the divine process as a multifaceted spectrum of wholeness, which at one end appears as the conventional world we all recognize, full of seemingly disparate objects, and at the other end lies the ultimate non-duality, where all multiplicity and separation are merely illusion.

The fourfold nature of God can be thought of as an aggregate of a number of divine phenomena. In it, the nature of God is perceived at various times as the empty ground of being and the physical world as we know it. Moreover, each world is itself also a process in which a different aspect of divine essence manifests. The explication of divine essence as process can be linguistically represented by using gerunds, words ending in "ing." "God" or "the Divine" is no longer viewed as a subject or a noun, but as a process and flow. This flow includes knowing, understanding, loving, and sensing.

This chart summarizes some of the teachings of the four worlds model as expressed by earlier generations of Jewish mystics:

Letter	Sound	Hebrew	Divine Manifestation	World Name	Soul Name
Not of the four worlds: *Yechidah* (singularity)					
Yud	y	י	Being	Atzilut	Chayah
Hay	h	ה	Knowing	Beriyah	Neshama
Vav	v	ו	Feeling	Yetzirah	Ruach
Hay	h	ה	Making/Doing	Assiyah	Nefesh

See practice 1 in the appendix to remind yourself of building a relationship to this fourfold model based on YHVH. One interesting teaching can be seen in the graphic of the Hebrew letters of this divine name, *Yud Hay Vav Hay*, when they are written from top to bottom.

Normally, Hebrew is written from left to right. However, when these letters are written one on top of the other, the resulting picture looks like a stick figure of a human being. This is a physical rendering of the line of Torah that says human beings are created in God's image. "God said: Let us make humankind in our image" (Genesis 1:26). Looked at it this way, the *yud* on top is like the head. The upper *hay* has the shape of shoulders and arms hanging down. The *vav* is the trunk or spine. And the lower *hay* is like the pelvis and legs. Each one of us is a hologram of the Divine. This metaphor need not be taken too literally but rather as a teaching that points in the direction that the Divine is to be found here in all of creation. And every person we encounter in our lives is an embodiment of the divine process.

The chart above summarizes some teachings of the Jewish mystics with regard to YHVH. What I would like to present is an explanation of their system that is not theoretical alone, but instead is integrated with my actual experience. The mystics chose their models by referring back to the primary Torah texts they believed contained secrets for understanding how God "Gods" the universe. Keep in mind that their loyalty to the actual verses of Torah led them to try to reconcile numerous verses to fit a model consistent with a legal view of Torah and ritual observation. They also believed in a oneness expressed through multiple worlds.

World Names

The names of the worlds come from Isaiah 43:7, "Everything was called into being [*atzilut*] through My name. For My glory I have created [*beriyah*] it, I have formed [*yetzirah*] it, even made [*assiyah*] it."[1] The mystics claim that this verse refers to the four worlds implied in the four-letter name YHVH and to something beyond it as well. That which is beyond the four worlds cannot be referred to conceptually. In that sense, "ineffable" takes on a meaning beyond mere ignorance of the correct pronunciation of YHVH; instead, it now has the connotation that language is inadequate to describe "That Which Is Beyond." This is the quality of the Divine captured by the Hebrew phrase *Ein Sof* (limitless, boundless), a Hebrew reference to that aspect of Divinity that is beyond the created universe. See my discussion of *Yechidah* below

Generally, when we say that we have a soul, we recognize that there is an outward manifestation of who we are and that there is also some inner spiritual reality ("soul" is here like a shorthand for this inner spiritual nature). In the mystics' model, there are four worlds of outer appearance, and each of them also has an inner, spiritual dimension. Traditionally, this inner dimension has often been seen as the God piece. However, our approach is based on the premise that "everything is God"; so, rather than saying that only the inner dimension is divine, we may rather see the outward aspect as the mundane manifestation of the Divine. The divine nature may appear less obvious here; yet underlying all mundane appearances there is sacredness or holiness in all things. For me, the primary distinction between the mundane world and sacredness is in the awakened nature of the consciousness that is beholding whatever has manifested. Each soul nature may represent a different aspect of the inner reality. And yet, as aspects of the Divine Unfolding, they also transcend any separation.

Nefesh, *ruach*, and *neshamah* are all soul/spirit words in Hebrew, and you see them as the soul names of the three lower worlds. In Hebrew these are all words related to wind and breath. English has a similar usage with the word "spirit," as in "respiration." The wind/breath nature of spirit connected to each of these realms captures the sense of flowing in and out that is common to all three worlds. It correlates to their shared reality of impermanence.

The World of *Assiyah*

Referring back to the chart, we'll work from the so-called bottom up, more or less. It's important to keep in mind that there is no linear progression here; in my reading, the relationship of *Yud Hay Vav Hay* is neither linear nor directional, there is no up or down or higher and lower—they are simply parts of a whole. This view is different from that of earlier generations of Jewish mystics, who did operate with a more hierarchical understanding of this process.

The world of the "lower" *hay* is called *Assiyah*, which is derived from the Hebrew word for "to do" or "to make." Both are good descriptions for this world: when something is made, it has become manifest. The worlds that have come into being are all part of what is made, or *Assiyah*. It's important not to get stuck in thinking that what has been made is static. Things come into being only temporarily. This is the truth of impermanence. *Assiyah* is the "world" where that which is temporarily manifesting is acted upon by everything else that is temporarily manifesting, and in that sense it is a realm of doing, where everything affects (does something to) everything else. Since it is always in flux, *Assiyah* can be referred to as *relative reality*. It is not absolute, because of its impermanence and constant change. It is better called *relative reality* in that everything is unfolding relative (in relationship) to everything else that is unfolding. We can also call it *conditional reality*. Everything that is manifest is manifest because of the conditions in everything else that are manifesting and because of the interplay of these conditions.

It is key to the theology of the four worlds model that *Assiyah* is understood as an aspect of the Divine Unfolding. It is not outside or separate from the Divine. And while everything in *Assiyah* is constantly changing, in any given moment, everything that is, is part of the Oneness of Being or Being Unfolding or God Wrapped in Robes of God. When we pay attention to the truth of what is—in this moment—we are attending to the Divine.

Nefesh is the Hebrew word for the soul/spirit name of the world of *Assiyah*. *Nefesh* can be seen as the animating force of the physical universe. Jewish mystics see it as a perpetual infusion of divine energy that keeps physicality in existence. I believe the authors of the Torah relate the breath with being born or created by God because every human being intuitively knows that breathing is a sign of aliveness. As mentioned earlier regarding the creation of the human being, living is an aspect of both *neshamah* and *nefesh*: "[God] breathed into [the human being's] nostrils the breath of life [*nishmat chayyim*] and the human became a living being [*l'nefesh chayah*]" (Genesis 2:7); the result is the "*neshamah* of life" residing inside this "living *nefesh* [the human]." Human beings create a sense of a world where life and breath are synonymous. *Nefesh* is the divine life force or soul name of the world of *Assiyah*. It exists as an embodied function of the life force (*chayah*), not separate from it (*nefesh chayah* means "a breathing aspect of life").

The World of *Yetzirah*

The second world in the chart above is referred to as *Yetzirah* and is associated with the letter *vav* in the tetragrammaton.

In the four worlds model, the association of the *vav* with *Yetzirah* is indicative of its "forming" nature. As the connecting force of Being Unfolding, *Yetzirah* is the force behind the process of combining and recombining that which has become manifest; it connects things to each other and thereby allows for them to be formed and reformed.

Ruach is the spiritual aspect of the *vav* or the connective aspect of Being Unfolding. *Vav* means "and" or "hook" in Hebrew. I think it is helpful to use a primal image from another tradition to understand the place of the *vav* in this model. Picture a yin-yang symbol (at right).

Imagine the intersection between the black and the white sections as a line that looks like this:

In this picture, the sine wave is like the *vav* that connects the *hay* on both sides of it in the *Yud Hay Vav Hay*. (The letter *yud* is like the black point in the white section or the white point in the black section.) Imagine that line to be neither black nor white but rather the "and" linking these two manifestations and bringing them into a greater unity. That connection is flowing like a wave; the boundary between the apparent twosome is fluid. I will explore the connective function in more depth in the final chapters of this book.

The outer manifestation of *Yetzirah* is its formative/connecting nature, and its inner dimension is called *ruach*. In our practical experience, we can best understand *ruach* as love. It is love that brings everything together. I see love as intrinsic to something that God is, not merely something that God does (its manifestation as the doing aspect is *Assiyah*). In the tetragrammaton, it is positioned right at the center or at the heart of the word. (Remember that in Hebrew, words have three-letter roots. In the tetragrammaton, the three-letter root is *hay-vav-hay*, and the *vav* is the middle letter of that root. Taken as a whole, the meaning of *hay-vav-hay* is the verb "to be.") Moreover, *ruach* appears in Torah before *neshamah* or *nefesh* is mentioned, even before anything else in the story that came into being.

In the first chapter of Genesis we read: *V'ruach Elohim m'rachefet al p'nay hamayim*, "The *ruach* aspect of *Elohim* hovering over the face of the water" (Genesis 1:2, my translation). *Ruach* was present before the first instance of speech (when God said, "Let there be light," in Genesis 1:3). Before any separation (man-made) came into being, love was hovering over the undifferentiated universe.

The world of the *vav* can be experienced in contemplation through practice 3, "The Power of 'And,'" in the appendix. If you can find a partner, you might want to try it now; or you can do it whenever the opportunity presents itself. The practice offers a way to get to a deeper appreciation of this world.

The World of *Atzilut*

As mentioned earlier, Jewish mystics traditionally assumed a linear unfolding of the four worlds, beginning with *Atzilut* and ending with *Assiyah*, or the physical world. The fact that *chayah*—life—is associated with *Atzilut* is an assertion of the fact that all realms fall under the umbrella of "life." All the manifest universe, everything that has come into being, is alive, and God is the source of life: "For with You is the source of life" (Psalm 36:10, my translation). In Jewish liturgy (see *Yishtabach* in the morning prayers), God is sometimes referred to as *chay ha-olamim*, which means "the life force of all worlds."

This understanding of life differs significantly from how, say, biologists define life. Conventionally, atoms are not considered alive, but when they eventually unite into larger patterns, we do call them alive. Of course, there are distinctions that can be made in how aliveness manifests in atoms versus plants versus animals versus human beings; yet, in line with Jewish mysticism, I consider all of these things alive. In fact, Judaism uses the metaphor of the Tree of Life to describe all that we call "existence" as manifestation of the Divine.

Atzilut refers to the realm of the non-dual. As mentioned, the Hebrew word implies no separation. If one object is next to another—that is, not separated—the term *aytzel* is used. It can also mean "with," as in *aytzli* (with me). Keep in mind that the original Jewish mystics did not go as far as later mystics in saying that "everything is God." The term *atzilut* still carries overtones of dualism in that it describes getting right next to God, allowing for a distinction between God and that which has come close to God. The notion of "nothing but God" was not popularized until the Baal Shem Tov's teachings in the eighteenth century.

Similarly, the term *devekut* (cleaving) was often seen as the purpose of mystical practice; Jewish mystics believed they must try to cleave to the Divine. However, in terms of the contemporary mysticism of this work, *devekut* needs to be understood differently. Rather than practicing in order to draw nigh to the Divine, in this approach *devekut* means a sustained awakening to the reality of interconnectedness.

In the context of my own contemplative practice, I equate the world of *Atzilut* with the awareness aspect of the Divine. Awareness has been compared to the open space of sky. Just as the clouds move through without affecting the sky, so too objects arise in awareness and pass through without affecting the awareness itself. And like open space, awareness has no outside and no inside; it contains all things without being limited or defined by them.

Awareness is a quality that is ever present. It is not exactly a part of conditioned reality, but rather the knowing of the conditional. In that sense, it is not impermanent. In contemplative practice, we can attune to the reality of awareness by "being the knowing." We can rest in the knowing of the objects of our awareness as they are coming and going. It is my experience and belief that this awareness is not me or mine. Sometimes an experience of "me and mine" arises and can then be known in awareness, but it's only a transitory object and not the subject that's "doing" the awareness; I say "sometimes" because in my personal experience this happens somewhat infrequently.

As amazing a phenomenon as awareness is, it is almost completely ignored precisely because it is ever present. There is no space between "me" and awareness, because that which is experienced as "me" arises within awareness. The Divine couldn't get closer to me, since it is aware of, and knowing the universe through, my senses. Jewish mystics sometimes call this realm *ayin*, "nothingness," and say it has the aroma of *Ein Sof*, the non-finite or infinite. Similarly, the Buddha called awareness a taste of the unborn, the uncreated, the unformed, the unconditioned.

The term *chayah* (life) is used synonymously for this realm. Unlike the realms of *Yetzirah* and *Assiyah*, which have clearly dualistic aspects, it does not make sense to call *chayah* an inner aspect and *Atzilut* an outer aspect of this world. But it is pleasing to me that "life" is one of the terms used to describe this realm, and all the other realms are sub-aspects of the Unfolding of Life.

Please look at practice 4 in the appendix. In contemplative practice, it is possible to emphasize resting in the field of awareness rather than focusing on the objects arising and passing within awareness.

The World of *Beriyah*

I have saved our discussion of the term *beriyah* (creating) for last, because this piece of my interpretation differs the most from the traditional understanding of Jewish mysticism. Key to my approach is the difference between "forming" (*yetzirah*) and "creating" (*beriyah*). In Hebrew, an artist is called a *yotzer*—a term implying that an artist, rather than "creating," is actually "forming" something out of existing material. In everyday parlance of art as a creative process, this distinction often falls away, but it is important in the context of our four worlds model. Traditionally, Judaism frequently refers to God as the creator of all things. This is the more traditional approach to the first line of the Torah that we looked at in chapter 1. *B'reshit bara Elohim et hashamayim v'et ha-aretz* (Genesis 1:1) is generally understood to mean "God created the heavens and earth." In this sense, God is the creator or that which caused that beginning. But we also find God referred to as the "former" or "shaper" of all that is, the *yotzer b'reshit*, in the *Aleynu* prayer at the end of Jewish prayer services. With this language we can avoid speculation on whether what we call God—a human concept—actually created existence or *is* Existence, which includes formative processes. Notice that *HaVaYaH*, made up of the same letters as YHVH, means "existence" in Hebrew.

The Jewish mystics commonly understood creation as the process of coming into being out of nothingness, *creatio ex nihilo*. However, in my interpretation *b'reshit* is not simply describing some original act of creation, but rather it is about the reshaping of our perceptions of reality that arose when conceptual thinking was formed (*yetzirah*) from the previously existing material of the universe. Perhaps all concepts can be called "creations" in that they come out of emptiness or nothingness. All "worlds" as described in the four worlds model are conceptual creations; we can see them as models or metaphors that help us understand how we perceive Being Unfolding. But these models—like all other models—also affect us and influence the way we shape (*yetzirah*) life. Words, opinions, and beliefs provide different lenses; they frame realities. Traditional Jewish mystics believe that God's words are the building blocks of the universe. By contrast, I don't believe words "create" new realities, but they impact the shaping or forming of reality. So powerful are our concepts and beliefs that the reality maps they create exist in a realm different from that which they purport to describe. They form a separate world called *Beriyah*. All of creation—all of what forms the world of *Beriyah*—is hence human-made.

This is a somewhat radical claim, as it seems to obliterate the notion of a Creator as the primary cause that brought everything into being. However, my intention is not to make any claims about such a first cause. I certainly don't know anything more about that than anyone else, and I am not even attempting to address the question. As I mentioned in my explanation of the opening chapters of Genesis, what I am interested in is the "coming into being" of human consciousness. With that came the stories, and Genesis is the product of an evolution of the early stories about creation.

These early creation stories (just like all stories) come into being through the conceptualizing mind. They have no more than a whiff or a flavor of some underlying reality (which is what contemplative practice opens us to). They are a bit like a dream in which some huge story is going on. Once we wake up, that story tends to fade away, because it never really happened. Still, it is fascinating to explore the process of story making, or *beriyah*; after all, it's key to being human.

We live in worlds that are made up of the stories we ourselves fabricate. But even though they are largely illusions, they do mirror reality—if only in a distorted way. The nature of how they came to be can tell us something about the deepest truths we need to know in order to live richer, fuller lives that are grounded in the actual way things are.

Now that we have looked at some of the limitations of the name for this world, let's investigate its profound spiritual significance. The reality maps of *Beriyah* can be generated by the deepest connection to intuitive wisdom, reflecting non-dual reality. The inner spiritual dimension of *Beriyah* is called *neshamah*. This dimension holds an aspect we can call wisdom or intuitive insight, which is able to discern the truths reflected in the stories we tell. As long as we are able to see the principles behind our story creations, it is possible not only to uncover the bits and pieces of truth and beauty in them, but also to transcend those aspects responsible for our sense of separation and alienation. From this perspective, *neshamah* is the process of insight, the process of acquiring intuitive wisdom. As we develop wisdom, we begin to see what's underneath our stories and the illusion of separateness.

Yechidah (Singularity)

When discussing the four worlds, Jewish mystics generally reference a fifth aspect called *yechidah*. In the approach I am teaching here, it references the aspect of the Divine that is not within the realm of four worlds of manifestation. As such, it is outside the conceptual. Whatever we say about it is by definition not it, since those references can only be made through concepts. In classical Jewish philosophy one might say *yechidah* can only be pointed to through the *via negativa*. We may say it is not manifest, not made of things not bounded (*ein sof*), and so on. While I believe we may intuit something outside our direct experience, I choose not to discuss it more in the context presented here, since such discussion could only be misleading.

The Fourfold Nature of Jewish Mindfulness Meditation

Mysticism can be defined as the direct experiencing of the Divine. From the perspective that everything is God and nothing but God, *all* direct experience is an experience of the Divine. The text above attempts to describe this as a fourfold process. But we can also directly access the four aspects through our experience. I invite you to try it and see for yourself.

When I pay attention to my direct experience, moment by moment, I am likely to notice a number of bodily sensations. Each of these sensations is created from contact between one of our senses and a sense object. The sense objects, say sounds or smells, are physical manifestations that are directly knowable. In our experiencing of them, we can distinguish three different events. One event is a knowing process; a second event is that knowing process coming into contact or connection with that which is being known; the third is the object that is being known.

Let's try this! As a test, pay attention to the sensations in your feet. Notice if there is the experience of pressure (usually categorized under the sense of touch) at certain places on the bottom of your feet. The sensory nature of life allows the knowing of the sense of touch. The sensations of the physical objects touching your feet (your socks, or pressure from the hardness of the floor) are the objects being known. The instruction to notice your feet likely caused you to direct your attention to that area of your body, and this allowed for a connection to be made between the knowing faculty and the particular sense objects around the feet.

Whatever can be known arises and passes in awareness. In order for things to be experienced in awareness, some process of attending must take place (Loving Attention). This is the function that connects that which can attend with that which can be attended to. This attending function is also an aspect of the Divine.

The experience of knowing is an amazing reality. It is an aspect of the Divine and so omnipresent that we tend to completely ignore it (as we do with anything that is omnipresent to our nervous systems). Part of what makes it so amazing is the fact that it's not a function of the "small I"; it's not something I produce or create. "Knowing" or "awareness" manifests through this form I call my body—but it's not manufactured by me. It is omnipresent and omnitemporal.

There is a fourth quality that I directly experience when I pay close attention. As I attend to various phenomena, clarity can arise as a result of that attention, an understanding of the nature of the phenomena and their relationships to each other. This clarity is wisdom, and its arising is another aspect of the Unfolding of Being that manifests in awareness. It is another aspect of the Divine, thus completing a picture of four interrelated divine phenomena, all of which can directly be part of our experience.

Part III

Coming to the Revelation at Sinai

5

The Human Journey

Perhaps it is the very nature of life's struggles that motivates us as human beings to begin the path to liberation. There is a call to practice that precedes awakening, and preceding the call to practice are the events that lead us to hear that call. When the awakening at Sinai occurred, it took place only after a spiritual journey that had been in process for a long time. In fact, that very journey began at the time of the expulsion from the Garden of Eden. The origin of human history (at the arrival or coming into being of conceptual thinking) contains within it the seeds for awakening. The stories of Genesis show the first fruits of these seeds and foretell a spiritual life that will eventually grow and prepare us for the resolution that is introduced in the experiences at Sinai. The earliest struggles are simultaneously the first steps on the path to liberation.

The Exodus is couched in the language of liberation for the Hebrew people. But the struggles are universal, and its message applies to each individual. We all must make the journey for ourselves. Awakening is a group project—but each of us has to do our own part and make our unique contribution. The Torah offers teachings about this journey. I imagine its authors were real people who essentially faced the same issues we do and who had their own set of spiritual practices. Their aspiration was to develop a relationship to something bigger than themselves, something divine (called by various names). The stories compiled in Genesis and Exodus describe the problem, the struggle to face it, and the arrival at a solution.

The Jewish description of this journey begins with the story of the first tribal patriarch, Avram, the "great father" (*av*, "father"; *ram*, "great"). I don't believe that this story is primarily designed to be about a particular person called Avram. Thinking of Avram as "our" particular ancestor can, in fact, be rather chauvinistic and has led some Jewish communities to believe that Jews are "the chosen people." Rather, the story of Avram, of the Great Father, is one of a prototypical journey, the kind of path each of us will have to take if we all want to wake up from confusion and alienation.

Perhaps all this is already hinted at in the Hebrew letters for "Great Father." The move from the non-dual (or pre-dual) to the dual is the move from one to two, from *aleph* to *bet*. Those are the two letters that make up the word *av*. (*Bet* is the same letter as *vet*, and it has these two possible pronunciations.) The word "father" could thus be an indication that the move to dualistic thinking is what "fathered" (that is, was the cause of) the need for the journey we all must take.

The very first thing we learn about Avram's life (other than his genealogy) is that YHVH speaks to him and tells him to go on a journey.

> YHVH said to Avram:
> Go-you-forth
> from your land,
> from your kindred [birthplace],
> from your father's house,
> to the land that I will let you see.
> GENESIS 12:1

At the time Avram receives this message, he doesn't have the knowledge or perspective about God that would later be revealed at Sinai. Even though the text says that YHVH spoke to him, Avram doesn't even know YHVH by that "name": "And I appeared unto Abraham, unto Isaac, and unto Jacob, as *El Shaddai*, but by My name YHVH I made Me not known to them" (Exodus 6:3, my translation). Yet, he does hear/feel a calling to look for more meaning in life. I imagine most of us feel such a calling, and so did the authors of the Torah. They knew from experience that to find meaning, often one must take a journey.

The midrash, a commentary on the Torah written by the early Rabbis of Judaism, tells us a story of the events that preceded this journey, the seeds, if you will:

Abraham's father, Terach, was an idol-manufacturer. Once he had to travel, so he left Abraham to manage the shop. People would come in and ask to buy idols.

Abraham would say, "How old are you?" The person would say, "Fifty," or "Sixty." Abraham would say, "Isn't it pathetic that a man of sixty wants to bow down to a one-day-old idol?" The man would feel ashamed and leave.

One time a woman came with a basket of bread. She said to Abraham, "Take this and offer it to the gods."

Abraham got up, took a hammer in his hand, broke all the idols to pieces, and then put the hammer in the hand of the biggest idol among them.

When his father came back and saw the broken idols, he was appalled. "Who did this?" he cried.

"How can I hide anything from you?" replied Abraham calmly. "A woman came with a basket of bread and told me to offer it to them. I brought it in front of them, and each one said, 'I'm going to eat first.' Then the biggest one got up, took the hammer, and broke all the others to pieces."

"What are you trying to pull on me?" asked Terach. "Do they have minds?"

Said Abraham: "Listen to what your own mouth is saying. They have no power at all! Why worship idols?"[1]

For me, the central message of the story is that to start our personal journey we must begin by breaking our parents' idols. As mentioned earlier, the story does not appear in the Torah text itself but in a Rabbinic interpretation of Genesis 12:1. It is part of a collection of stories about the Torah that was verbally passed down for hundreds of years before it was recorded in the third century in Palestine. Around the start of the Common Era, two thousand years ago, Rabbinic Judaism began to replace the older system of priestly Judaism. Perhaps the tale served as an early justification for the Rabbis to rework the Jewish tradition of their ancestors. But whatever its historical background, the story has an important message. It tells us that to find our true self, we have to first leave behind our conditioning.

The story of Avram is generally understood to be the beginning of the Hebrew people, but I believe it offers a more general lesson. As mentioned above, Avram's tale begins with "God" telling Avram to take a journey. The Hebrew words are *lech lecha* (Genesis 12:1). *Lech* in Hebrew is the imperative form of the verb "to go." The second word is a construct in Hebrew, which generally means "to you." The letter *lamed*, with the sound of an "L" in English, means "to" or "toward" and can be declined in Hebrew with different endings to mean "to me," "to you," "to him," "to her," and so on. Most translators take this to mean something like "go-you-forth" (Fox) or "get thee out" (Soncino). But the literal translation can be read as meaning that Avram is being told to "get going to yourself."

In order to "get going," Avram, meaning each one of us, must depart from our "land," from our "birthplace," and from our "parent's house." If indeed our beginning task is to get back to ourselves, to our true selves, then we have to leave behind everything that has conditioned us to conform to generally held beliefs, views, and opinions. The above categories (land, birthplace, parent's house) cover the most profound factors that shape our usual identities. They are the prototypical conditions that tend to restrict the possibility of a journey of discovery. "Land" refers to our cultural conditioning, the impact of our particular culture and subculture. These cultures and subcultures include (but are not limited to) nationality, national religion, class, politics, neighborhood, and some aspects of gender. "Birthplace" refers to the conditions that come as a result of taking birth in our human form and with our genetic inheritance. For example, we each have nervous systems and certain senses, we lust after pleasant conditions and avoid or become angry at unpleasant conditions, and so on. Finally our "parent's house" refers to the conditioning more particular to our unique situations and personal identity; this might include the customs of our family of origin such as family religion, guild membership, and a wide range of acquired personal traits such as fearfulness, a critical disposition, anger, insecurity, acceptance, kindness, and so on. The story of Avram tells us that it is necessary to leave all this behind if we seek to find our true selves.

Now let's take a look at the first two words YHVH said to Avram: *Lech lecha*, לֶךְ-לְךָ, and to what those two words could be pointing us toward. What does it mean to go to yourself? Isn't it the case that wherever you go, there you are? Why do you need to go anywhere in the first place? Is it perhaps because you may not be who you think you are? Illuminating all of the above-mentioned conditioning for what it is—simply conditioning, rather than a genuine part of our true selves—is for many one of the greatest challenges of our spiritual journey.

Most of us have a strong sense of self-identity, and we tend to be very attached to this identity. I have heard Bernie Glassman, a noted Zen teacher, start off his teaching by saying, "Hi, I'm Bernie, and I'm an addict. I'm addicted to being Bernie." Bernie is pointing out the nature of being addicted or attached to our views and beliefs about who we think we are. This notion of self comprises the qualities and characteristics we tend to think of as residing in our physical bodies. But maybe we have had wrong ideas about the true qualities and characteristics of our self. Maybe we should go back to reconsider what they really are.

Another interpretation is that our journey to find enlightenment naturally leads us back to our starting point: ourselves. Even if we don't know any Hebrew, we can immediately see that the two words לך–לך look identical. (Remember, in the Torah, Hebrew letters are written without vowels or punctuation; the pronunciation is based on knowledge of the Hebrew language and initially upon oral traditions. Only later was a system of vocalization created and standardized texts written down with the "correct" or "official" pronunciations. The pronunciation *lech lecha* goes back to this convention, but originally the words themselves were identically written.) Maybe this points to a truth about ourselves and our journey. Maybe the journey doesn't really change the qualities and characteristics of ourselves. Maybe it doesn't change who we are as much as it changes how we perceive and understand ourselves through a deepened awareness.

While these interpretations can help open our mind, they are still somewhat limited by the traditional ways of looking at the text. My own understanding is different in that I believe the duplication of the letters strongly hints at something else. I think it points us to seeing the destination as a verb rather than a noun.

The "destination" ("to yourself") is identical to the process of "going" ("get going"). After all, there is no destination to reach because we are something that is continually in the process of going, always in flux, always a being unfolding. In other words, we are not the thing that gets unfolded, but the process of unfolding itself. What we usually consider to be our self is no more than a snapshot of a constantly moving, always changing process. That is the change in awareness that the journey can awaken.

My children once told me a joke that speaks to this understanding. "You go into the bathroom and you are an American. When you come out of the bathroom, you are an American. What are you while you are in the bathroom? European ("You're a peein'")." The joke hits upon the reality that each of us really is a "walking," a "breathing," a "sleeping," an "eating," a "thinking." The one thing that we are not is something solid, fixed, or unchanging. The true self is that which is the process of being unfolded.

Our habitual sense of identity masks this. We use mental labels to create identities, such as "I am a male rabbi," "a teacher," "a father," etc. A better description would depict me as engaged in rabbi-ing, expressing gender, teaching, parenting, and so on. And even at that, those actions change over time, arising and ceasing and transforming—they are not all happening at once.

Avram's story of leaving home strongly resonates with my personal experience. My own journey to finding my true self began when I left my parents' house. It was during my junior year in high school, a time to begin planning for college, when my father and my mother's uncle Eddie sat me down to talk about careers. Both my parents were first-generation Americans (their parents being from Russia), so none of my grandparents had been to college. Uncle Eddie had been the only one of that generation who managed to attend college. Essentially he'd "made it" in America, so my father had invited him to consult on my career choices (Eddie had also mentored my father twenty-five years earlier). For my father's part, his family had been too poor to afford higher education for any of their children, but World War II and the GI Bill changed his fate and made it possible. Under Eddie's guidance my father had gone to Marquette University, where he studied to become an accountant.

The day the two of them sat me down to discuss my future, they told me to be an accounting major in college, get CPA certification, and then go on to law school to become a tax attorney. ("Tax attorneys make much more money than CPAs.") After that, I could go into business with my father. It sounded like a good plan to me. Since I grew up in Milwaukee in an upper-middle-class suburb with a large Jewish population, it was assumed I would go to college and that there were three basic options for a son's career: to become a lawyer or a doctor or to go into business with his father. It was simply the way it was, and (almost) all my friends and acquaintances did exactly that.

I arrived at the University of Wisconsin in the fall of 1970, in the midst of the war in Vietnam. The university was a hotbed of antiwar activism. All I knew about the war was that it was based on some vague domino theory that claimed if Vietnam fell to the communists, other countries would soon fall to communism as well. That, it was said, needed to be stopped at nearly any cost. Frankly, I hadn't been paying much attention. I was too busy playing basketball and leading my Jewish youth group, B'nai B'rith Youth Organization. As I began to learn more about the war though, I felt it was wrong (likely an aversive mental pattern arising out of fear of the draft), and I began planning to make a case for conscientious objector status. As it turned out, the draft lottery assigned such a high number to me that there was virtually no chance of my being called up for service. But what I learned about the war in Vietnam greatly influenced my outlook on life. It was my first experience of awakening from preconditioned beliefs. I realized that what was happening to poor people on the other side of the world was directly related to my own privilege and to actions of the people and government of my country. I felt there was need for a revolution in both our values and our lifestyle. I simply couldn't go through with the career plan my father and my great-uncle had designed for me, becoming an accountant and a part of the capitalist "ruling class." In a way, I needed to break my father's idols, although back then I would not have used that metaphor.

It was extremely difficult for me to tell my father that I was dropping out of my introductory accounting class. First, he tried to convince me to put the decision off, and when he couldn't persuade me, he appealed to our personal relationship. "Please, do it for me," he said. "Just finish the course for me." It was as powerful a moment as it was painful, and I remember crying as I told him that I was sorry, but I just couldn't do that. He was so hurt that he stopped speaking to me for about three weeks. Even today, I can't *quite* look at it as "smashing his idols." I didn't think my father was doing something wrong; in fact, I was always proud of him for his accomplishments. I just knew it couldn't be my path. I can imagine though that for him it felt like his dreams for me were being smashed.

Of course, leaving our parents' home and way of life is not *automatically* the beginning of our own journey. Conditioning is a powerful force that needs to be understood and recognized before it can be managed. When I dropped accounting, I switched to pre-med, believing that this was now my own choice. Little did I understand then that even this new "choice" was just another result of my conditioning, that is, the belief that the only three options available to me were accounting, law, and medicine. Sometimes it is difficult to recognize what binds us even if we are trying to break free. Also, conditioning isn't something that can be broken all at once and permanently. We need to continually reevaluate our path. The Jewish practice of the High Holy Days, an annual occasion for examining one's life, is a good tool to help us with this task. Shabbat practice offers time for weekly reflection on our life's journey.

Let's look back at Avram's story in the midrash. Now that we know we need to question our conditioning and maybe even smash our father's idols, perhaps it would help to better understand what those idols are. What is an idol? (Anything worshiped is sometimes called an idol, but another sense of the term is an image or a representation that is worshiped, and that is how I am using the term.) Simply put, idols have two characteristics: (a) they are formed by human beings; (b) they are worshiped by human beings. A statue is not an idol if no one worships it, and something, even if it is worshiped, is not necessarily an idol unless made by human beings. Only when both aspects come together can we use the language of idolatry. We human beings make our beliefs, views, and opinions, but that doesn't make them idols. Only when we start worshiping them does the process becomes idolatrous. A "nation" may be a skillful means of gathering like-minded people together in various social structures, but worshiping a nation seems to me idolatrous. The use of money as a means to exchange goods may be a fine system, but worshiping money and wealth is idolatrous. I think these two qualities—being made by humans and being worshiped by humans—are at the core of Judaism's rebuke of idolatry.

Unfortunately, we often overlook the fact that much of what we worship (and much of what other organized religions worship) was fashioned by human beings. This includes names for God and fixed beliefs in what God is or wants. Human beings created language, culture, society, religion, and so on, as well as sense of self. There is nothing inherently wrong with creating things if their creation is in the service of helping and supporting all beings. But when we start to lose sight of their true nature as human artifacts, when we start believing in them as independent realities that must be attained, valued, prayed to, and worshiped, that's when we fall under their spell, and they become fetters or chains that hold us back from our journey.

So, what is it that we might see when we actually do break those fetters and finally begin our journey? YHVH tells Avram to leave one land to go to another land, "the land that I will show you" (Genesis 12:1). But what is this other land? And who is the "I" that will show him (us) where to go? How does the showing process happen?

The "I" that does the showing is referred to at the beginning of the verse as YHVH, and as I have been suggesting earlier, YHVH is not a name but rather a placeholder for "Loving Attention to the Truth of what is Unfolding to and through the senses of the body, resulting in Arising Wisdom being known in Awareness." This is what shows us where our journey is heading. And this understanding of YHVH is also what we truly are. The "land" where we fully realize this is not a particular place somewhere else; it is right here and right now and in us. This is what we are being shown, this is what fulfills the promise of taking a journey, this is the "promised land." "YHVH said to Avram: Go-you-forth from your land, from your birthplace, from your father's house, to the land that I will show you" (Genesis 12:1).

With this understanding of "the land," the five books of the Torah tell of a journey quite different from what we may have previously thought. It is not about a people as a political entity looking to reclaim their ancestral homeland; the "promised land" is not some acreage in a particular part of the globe. Rather, it is about a homecoming to the here and now. The Torah can be seen as showing us a map that helps us navigate this terrain. Life is essentially wild, unfolding as it will, independent of our categorizations. The here and now is a wilderness, constantly changing, largely unpredictable, and ultimately out of our control. But the Torah can help us see a path.

The Torah also hints at another amazing aspect of the wilderness that we are all in at this moment. The Hebrew word the Torah uses for "wilderness" is *midbar*. The first letter of that word is *mem*. When a *mem* is appended to a three-letter root, it makes a new noun whose meaning is "the place where that root meaning happens." For instance, the root *k-d-sh* (*kuf-dalet-shin*) means "holy," and *mikdash* is the word for the sanctuary where the Holy Presence of the Divine dwells. The word *midbar* is the place where the root word *d-b/v-r* (*dalet-bet/vet-raysh*) occurs; it generally means "wilderness." The three-letter root *d-b/v-r* can mean "thing," "word," or "speech." When we are living in worlds made up of words, we are living in what Torah calls the wilderness. Living in reality maps that are created by human words, as discussed earlier, is nothing other than living in the wilderness.

It is not a "bad" thing that we live in that wilderness. It is simply the way things are in the here and now. It is where the journey of life, or Torah, takes place. That is what we are being shown through our practice of paying Loving Attention to our lives. We are "the land" that is shown to us, and we are the process that is doing this showing. Through paying Loving Attention we become aware of life in a way that can transcend our usual conditioning.

6

Toward a Culture of Holiness

The book of Exodus is a story of deliverance. On one level, it tells us about the liberation of the Hebrew people from their slavery in Egypt. But wrapped within this tale is another story, one that draws the outline of a new spiritual path for the Jewish people, a path that commissions the children of Israel to the fundamental task of repairing the rift in God, or the Unfolding of Being. I think this path leads to the creation of a culture of holiness. It applies to all people who are committed to waking up and contributing to a transformation in human consciousness.

Wrestling to Embrace the Divine at Our Core

When the Jewish people refer to themselves as "the children of Israel," this is a reference to themselves as the spiritual offspring of a transformative process that began when Jacob's name became Israel (Genesis 32).

The story begins when Jacob, son of Isaac, son of Abraham, is about to meet his older twin brother Esau for the first time since he'd fled their homeland. Jacob had stolen the blessing of the first-born from Esau by deceiving their father, and Esau had threatened to kill Jacob over the incident. Their mother, Rebecca, was afraid for Jacob's life, and warned him to escape. Years have now gone by, and both brothers have grown up and established significant households and are the tribal leaders of large clans. Nevertheless, Jacob remains concerned that Esau is still seeking revenge, so before the meeting takes place, he divides his clan in two. This way if one camp were to be attacked by Esau and his clan, at least the other would escape. With that finished, Jacob spends the night alone in preparation for the meeting.

> And Jacob was left alone, and a man wrestled with him until the break of dawn. When he saw that he could not [prevail] against him, he touched the socket of his hip, and the socket of Jacob's hip became dislocated as he wrestled with him. And he [the angel] said, "Let me go, for dawn is breaking," but he [Jacob] said, "I will not send you away unless you have blessed me." So he said to him, "What is your name?" and he said, "Jacob." And he said, "Your name shall no longer be called Jacob, but rather Israel, because you have wrestled with God and with men, and you have prevailed." And Jacob asked and said, "Now tell me your name," and he said, "Why is it that you ask for my name?" And [the angel] blessed him there. And Jacob called the name of the place Peniel, for [he said,] "I saw God face to face, and my soul was saved."[1]
>
> GENESIS 32:25–31

After living with the deed of his stolen blessing for so many years, Jacob has finally stopped running and is ready to face the consequences of his actions. We can only imagine the internal struggle he is going through! He must look deeply into his heart and come to terms with what is there. Perhaps this is hinted at through the number of the chapter in which the story appears, chapter 32. For Jewish mystics, the alphabetic representations of the number 32 are the Hebrew letters *lamed* and *bet*, which together form the word *lev* (heart). In Hebrew, the first ten letters, *alef* through *yud*, represent the numbers 1–10. The next eight letters, *kaf* through *tzadi* represent

20–90, and *kuf through tav* represent 100–400. In this example, *lamed* is the letter with the value of 30, and *bet*, being the second letter, is the number 2. When we look closely into our hearts, we are sometimes forced to look at the difficult feelings that are present. The imagery of wrestling captures this beautifully, as it is simultaneously one of intimate connection and struggle. Jacob prevails in his internal struggle, meaning he is not shutting off or ignoring what he finds in his heart, and as a result he is reborn a different man. There is no victor and no loser; the match concludes with a blessing. This blessing is contrasted with the one at the beginning of the story. It isn't stolen or even something that *can* be stolen. Rather, it comes from the work of fully and honestly facing the truth of the heart. Only when we do this can we start the process of transformation (as Jacob was transformed into Israel).

Folded into the text are more requests for names and name changes. As Arthur Waskow points out, the patriarch Yaakov (Jacob) wrestles (*va-yayavayk*) with an angel at the river Yabbok (Genesis 32:25), and those words play with the same syllables and in essence turns the names "inside out" and highlights the process of transformation and growth.[2] Jacob, when he prevails, is given a new name, Yisrael: "Your name shall no longer be called Jacob, but rather Israel, because you have wrestled with God and with men, and you have prevailed" (32:29). Yisrael is a construct of *Ysr-el*, with *ysr*, the verb "to strive," and *el*, a name for God, hence Waskow's term "Godwrestler." Now, if as I propose in this book, we look at God as the True Nature of Being (rather than a transcendent entity), then Jacob's accomplishment here is to have fully opened up to the True Nature of Being. Perhaps the name change to Yisrael isn't merely the creation of a new individual name then, but rather is a process term that can be applied to anyone who is looking deeply inside. Whenever we do this work, we are the children of Israel.

This work sets in motion the process that will heal the rift we have caused while living in the ignorance of separation. It begins the creation of a culture of holiness in the world. We lost (and continue to lose) our freedom when we became caught in the concepts and the narratives of small mind. In fact, I think this is precisely what Egypt represents. (We will look at Egypt and the story of Exodus in a moment.) As my friend and mindfulness teacher Sylvia Boorstein likes to say, "I descend into Egypt many times each day."

Creating a culture of holiness is what will deliver us. According to anthropologists, a culture is the sum of ways of living built up by a group of human beings and transmitted from one generation to the next. In concordance with this concept, I believe that the process of awakening is ultimately a collective endeavor. It takes a culture for us to free ourselves from our ignorance, from greed, and from hatred; it is also within a culture of holiness that we all can gain the wisdom and support to open our hearts and realize the interconnectivity of all that is.

The Torah represents the group efforts of at least some significant part of the Jewish people. It is a collective story, both in its origins and in the many lives it describes, as well as in the collective engagement with the scroll across generations of the children of Israel. While the practice of mindfulness is extremely valuable as an individual pursuit, it is also a central component in the creation of a worldwide culture of holiness. As such, it's key to the Jewish enterprise as a whole and, in my opinion, to every other culture as well.

The story in Genesis describes the origin of a culture of history. It describes the arising of conceptual thinking, which spawns many beautiful achievements and ideas, but also creates a sense of individual alienation that allows greed and hatred to enter human consciousness. This process eventually leads to the misery of everything that Egypt represents (to the individual and society). In the stories of Avram and then Jacob, we see the first seeds of transformation. But only in Exodus do we find the outline of a path to freedom through the creation of a culture of holiness, that is, a culture in which humans work together to create holiness.

Leaving Egypt for a Desert Retreat

The Hebrew people were divided into twelve tribes, each fathered by a son of the patriarch Jacob. The book of Exodus begins with the line, "Now these are names of the Children of Israel coming to Egypt, with [Jacob], each man and his household they came" (Exodus 1:1, my translation). Jacob is known by two names based on the earlier story of his wrestling with an angel—or some say a man—in which he acquires the name Israel. As Genesis ends, we learn that all the tribes left their homeland of Canaan to escape a famine. They initially fared well and began to prosper in Egypt. One son, Joseph, even became an assistant to the Pharaoh.

After some time, however, a new pharaoh arose "who knew not Joseph," and fearing that the Hebrew tribes might become a fifth column against him in his wars with neighboring countries, he enslaved the people. When he gave an order that all Jewish newborn sons be killed, one family tried to evade the order by sending their son in a basket down the river Nile. The young child was found by Pharaoh's daughter, who then named the little boy Moses and had him raised in the palace. As an adult, Moses learned of his origins and objected to the slavery of his people. Following an event in which he killed an Egyptian overseer, he fled Egypt to live in Midian, where he became a shepherd and married Tzipporah, the daughter of the priest of Midian. According to the story, he was forty years old when he left Egypt, and then he spent another forty years wandering in the wilderness. This is essentially a forty-year silent retreat. At this point an amazing event takes place, an event that initiates the essential, transformative path of Judaism: Moses's experience at the burning bush.

Forty is a symbolic number in Jewish teaching (also used, for example, in the story of the flood, when it rained for forty days), but what does that number symbolize exactly? When a woman conceives a child, it is approximately forty weeks from her last period until the birth occurs. Forty is hence the number that represents birth, a new dawning, the time it takes to mature from conception into a whole new being. So when Moses leaves Egypt at age forty, it signifies the end of one period and the arrival of a new beginning. And when we learn that Moses is eighty years old when he sees the burning bush, this again tells us that something new and eventful is about to unfold. In addition to the numerical symbolism, the fact that he had just spent forty years wandering in the wilderness as a shepherd made it likely that he'd be open to experiences outside the normal bounds of societal conditioning (that is, the conceptual thinking that is binding us). Wandering in the wilderness is a common theme for spiritual leaders. The Buddha leaves society behind for his transformations to occur. And we are told that the Baal Shem Tov also spent seven years journeying in the Carpathian Mountains, returning home only for Shabbat each week.

So let's look closely at what happened. Moses was shepherding the flock of his father-in-law, Jethro, when he came to the mountain of God, where YHVH's message was revealed to him in the form of a flame in the midst of a bush. To his surprise, he sees the bush is not consumed.

> ³ Moshe said:
>> Now let me turn aside
>> that I may see this great sight—
>> why the bush does not burn up!
> ⁴ When YHVH saw that he had turned aside to see,
>> God called to him out of the midst of the bush,
>> He said:
>> Moshe! Moshe!
>> He said:
>> Here I am.
> ⁵ He said:
>> Do not come near to here,
>> put off your sandal from your foot,
>> for the place on which you stand—it is holy ground!
>> Exodus 3:1–5

Considering the enormous importance of the burning bush narrative, we can appreciate the simple truths it offers in helping us recognize the Divine Presence in our own lives. Before Moses or any one of us is able to perceive holiness, we first must commit to "turn" and to "see" what life is revealing to us. Only when we stop heading in the same direction, when we turn and see, or pay attention, might we experience the Divine Presence. Moses becomes inquisitive about what he is experiencing, "that I may see this great sight—why the bush does not burn up." When we open up to our experience and become deeply interested in what we see, the experience itself begins to "speak" to us. And when it does, we need to show up, stay present, and say, "Here I am," to the experience. It is at this point that we can sometimes see the fire, the ever-flowing energy inherent in all of life. In essence, I believe that every "bush" (that is, every thing or event) we look at is on fire. And when we are awake we realize that we are fire (or on fire) as well. The fire outside is none other than the fire inside. That is why we can recognize it in those moments.

What Is Holiness?

It's important to note that here the term "holiness" is reintroduced into the narrative of the Torah. It was last mentioned at the very beginning of Genesis in connection with the seventh day, the Shabbat, prior to the incident of the humans eating from the Tree of the Knowing of Good and Evil. After that incident, the word "holy/holiness" is dropped. However, once the burning bush's location is called "holy ground," holiness becomes a defining term that is frequently used in relation to God and to the children of Israel, who enter into relationship with God. So let's pause for a moment and explore the term "holy" before continuing with the narrative.

In the lineage of the Jewish mystics, we can begin by deconstructing the word "holy" (*kadosh*). It must be understood in relation to its opposite term, "profane" (*chol*). The word *chalal* means "to bore a hole, to pierce." So, in Hebrew, the word *chalil* means "flute"—a reed with holes pierced in it. The term for "apostasy" in Hebrew is *chilul hashem,* which means "desecrating the name" or "profaning the name." What is the link between poking holes and desecrating a name? A name is a kind of interface between an object being known and the knower. We use names to make connections to the item that is being named. When a name is profaned, it loses its connective ability. Each time we use a name as a curse, we disrupt its connective nature, poke holes into it; the concept of profanation is hence linked to the idea of poking holes into something until it loses its integrity.

"Holiness" in its most basic use in biblical text refers to God's nature. God is holy, and anything connected to God is holy. Literally, in the above-mentioned Exodus verse, the ground is holy because God appears there. In Leviticus 19:2 we read: "You shall be holy, for I, YHVH your God, am holy." Again in Isaiah 6:3 we read: "Holy, holy, holy is YHVH of Hosts." So the word "holy" can be positively defined only in reference to God. But we can try to further understand it by clarifying what it is not, in contrast to the profane.

Traditionally, holiness is often understood as separateness. "You shall be holy: You should keep distant from sin and licentiousness, for wherever you find decrees against sexual misconduct you find holiness," comments Rashi on Leviticus 19:2. Rashi understands holiness as separating oneself from worldly conduct. Applying this to our verse, we may say that the holy ground was different or separate from any regular ground in that it was here that God was found. This concept of separateness as the defining quality of holiness is related to a belief of ultimate separateness between God and the world. When one's concept of the Divine is utterly transcendent, and separateness from worldly matters becomes the definition of "holy/sacred," then to act in holy ways means to leave the mundane world behind. This is the reason that *kiddush hashem*—literally, "sanctification of the divine name," the opposite of *chilul hashem,* "desecration of the divine name"—is a synonym for martyrdom. In order to honor God's holiness, you must literally die in this world.

Contrary to this traditional understanding, I believe that holiness needs to be transvalued for a generation of Jews who are contemporary mystics and who have a theology of radical monism when contemplating Being Unfolding. This theology is based on God's immanence in all Being—God's presence within, rather than God's separateness from.

The distinction between the sacred and the profane, then, I believe, is not one between transcendence and immanence, since God *is* actually immanent, but rather it is a reflection of the consciousness and attention that we bring to each moment. The ground where Moses sees the burning bush is made holy by the quality of consciousness Moses brings to the experience. His heart is open, his whole being is present, and he is fully aware and mindful, truly seeing what is happening at that moment. "When YHVH saw that he had turned aside to see, God called to him out of the midst of the bush" (Exodus 3:4). This quality of attention or mindfulness transforms the ground from a mundane location to holy ground; it is from this place that God calls out to Moses. Whenever we fully pay attention, we are connected to Being Unfolding.

We saw earlier that the root of the Hebrew word for "profane" goes back to "puncturing" or "making holes." We can now understand what this means. Holes are ruptures in the connections between things, places where gaps have opened and things are no longer joined. Going back to Rashi's understanding of sexual misconduct, the issue perhaps is not one of being involved with bodily rather than spiritual matters; rather, the issue could be that sexual misconduct punctures our connections to other living beings. Profane conduct is that which further reinforces our sense of separateness from other beings and from the Holy One of Being. Acting in holiness or sacredness would then be defined as cultivating the consciousness of the Interconnection of All Beings or All Being. In a reconceptionist approach, holiness is transformed from an expression of separateness from worldly matters to an expression of radical interconnection or non-separateness. This flows from the realization that everything is God and nothing but God.

A Wondrous Revelation Enters Human History

Now, let's return to our narrative. Since Moses has turned to attend to what was occurring in the present moment of being, he is able to hear the Divine. For Moses and for us, when we attend to the truth of what is in this present moment of experience, it is always a moment of non-separation. I think this is signified symbolically by the instruction to remove his shoes. Because this is "holy ground," we don't want anything between us and the ground. The shoes are akin to the many filters through which we usually perceive reality (even when we try to attend to the moment), filters such as desire, aversion, doubt, beliefs, ego identity, and so on. So, Moses is saying "Here I am" to the moment; just "here I am."

> [6] Moreover, He said: "I am the God of thy father, the God of Abraham, the God of Isaac, and the God of Jacob." And Moses hid his face; for he was afraid to look upon God.
>
> [7] And [YHVH] said: "I have surely seen the affliction of My people that are in Egypt and have heard their cry by reason of their taskmasters, for I know their pains;
>
> [8] and I am come down to deliver them out of the hand of the Egyptians, and to bring them up out of that land unto a good land and a large, unto a land flowing with milk and honey; unto the place of the Canaanite, and the Hittite, and the Amorite, and the Perizzite, and the Hivvite, and the Jebusite.
>
> [9] And now, behold, the cry of the children of Israel is come unto Me; moreover I have seen the oppression wherewith the Egyptians oppress them.
>
> [10] Come now therefore, and I will send thee unto Pharaoh, that thou mayest bring forth My people the children of Israel out of Egypt."

¹¹ And Moses said to God: "Who am I, that I should go unto Pharaoh, and that I should bring forth the children of Israel out of Egypt?"

¹² And He said: "Certainly I will be with thee; and this shall be the token unto thee, that I have sent thee: when thou hast brought forth the people out of Egypt, ye shall serve God upon this mountain."

¹³ And Moses said unto God: "Behold, when I come unto the children of Israel, and shall say unto them: The God of your fathers has sent me unto you; and they shall say to me: What is His name? what shall I say unto them?"

¹⁴ And God said unto Moses, "I am that I am (*Ehyeh asher ehyeh*)"; and He said: "Thus shalt thou say unto the children of Israel: I am (*Ehyeh*) hath sent me unto you."³

The revelation that happens at the burning bush begins with Moses being reminded of his ancestry, the descendants of whom are the people he has left behind and who have been living in slavery for the past forty years. Perhaps this experience of wrongful slavery is the fire that has been burning inside him all of this time, one he wasn't prepared to face—until this moment. Now, opening himself to the pain of it, he turns his head in shame: "And Moses hid his face; for he was afraid to look upon God" (Exodus 3:6). Looking at the truth—the naked truth—is not always easy.

The subsequent verses acknowledge that Moses is now fully aware of his people's affliction and that he has to act on it. He is commissioned to go to Pharaoh and deliver the children of Israel from Egypt back to the land of their origin. At this point, Moses's attitude shifts from "Here am I" to "Who am I?" Fear and doubt are arising in him. "Who am I, that I should go unto Pharaoh, and that I should bring forth the children of Israel out of Egypt?" (Exodus 3:11). God's response is, "Certainly I will be with thee; and this shall be the token unto thee, that I have sent thee" (3:12). It is worth exploring these two verses even though most people focus on the far more well-known verses 3:13–14. At first glance, it seems that the apparent meaning of the words in verse 12 don't provide much of an answer to Moses's question. He is asking about who he is and whether he is the right person for this task, but the response appears incongruent.

The Hebrew word *ehyeh* is used in God's response, and this word will reappear in the famous phrase to come. The Hebrew for "Because I will be with you" is *Kee ehyeh eemach* (Exodus 3:12). The Hebrew word *kee* means "because," *ehyeh* simply means "I will be," and *eemach* means "with you." The Hebrew word *ehyeh* is a construct form of the verb "to be" in the first person future tense form. In this form, an *aleph* is added before the root letters *hay-vav-hay*, which are the root letters for the verb "to be."

"I will be with you" does not seem to answer the question Moses asked, "Who am I?" Or does it? And what is the "sign" that God will be with Moses? Can the fact that God is with Moses be in itself a sign? Maybe we need to find another way to read these verses. The verb "to be" is not always necessary in a sentence; it can be simply implied. *Ehyeh* could, in fact, be a noun, which would render the reading of this phrase as *"Ehyeh* is with you." This clearly is what happens at the end of Exodus 3:14. There is no doubt that *ehyeh* is key to this passage. Perhaps God Godself is the answer to Moses's question "Who am I?" But let's not jump ahead of the story.

Just as it might seem to us that in Exodus 3:12 God has not answered Moses's question "Who am I?" so too Moses's doubt is not alleviated. There is one concern in his mind that seems particularly pressing for him. When he gets to Egypt to tell the children of Israel that the God of their fathers has sent him, they would surely ask him, "What's God's name [i.e., which God]?" And so, he inquires of God, how should he respond? What name should he give them?

Moses's question seems to refer back to a time when there were many gods with many names—every culture had their own gods. (To some extent, we may say that this is still true today.) The Hebrew people had their singular God (though it wasn't always known by the same name), but they were enslaved in Egypt, where those people had their own gods (Amon-Re, Horus, Osiris, Atum; the Pharaoh himself was considered to be a divine being), and political power was seen as a sign of God's providence. The mind-set of the ruling powers held that the Hebrew people were slaves because the god(s) of Egypt were more powerful than the God of the Hebrews. Accordingly, from the perspective of the biblical narrative, if Moses were to free the Hebrews, it had to be because God was using him as the agent to liberate them from a country that believed in false gods. Moses was not going to Pharaoh with an ethical case for the liberation of the Hebrew people from oppression, as just as that cause might have been. The writers of this narrative rather believed that divine forces were propelling the liberation.

Convinced that the God of the Hebrew people was behind the events that transpired, the authors set the stage for a battle between their God and the false gods of Egypt. And perhaps as a redeemer who came from that culture, Moses would have known that the faith of the slaves in their God was weakened by their oppression. He would have known that many had no faith in the power of their God. He would have known that they had been raised exposed to other gods who were associated with great, powerful Pharaohs and their armies. It was only natural that they were going to question him about the authority behind his efforts to liberate them.

With all this in mind, let's look at how the Torah narrative reports God's response to the question "I will say to them, 'The God of your fathers has sent me to you,' and they will say to me, 'What is [God's] name?'—what shall I say to them?" (Exodus 3:13). It is one of the most famous lines of the Torah and a statement of great significance.

God says *Ehyeh asher ehyeh*, "I am that I am" (Cohen), or "I will be-there howsoever I will be-there" (Fox). And then the Divine repeats, "Thus shall you say to the Children of Israel: *Ehyeh* / I-Will-Be-There sends me to you" (Exodus 3:14). This response is as astounding as it is puzzling, since it seems to deliberately ignore the request for a name. "I will be (there)" (*ehyeh*) certainly does not sound like a name. Furthermore, the fact that *ehyeh* is said twice in the initial response gives it the appearance of a declaration, an exclamation even: I am! I am!

Let me say a word about Hebrew before picking up on more of what this response might mean. Biblical Hebrew does not have past and future verb tenses but rather has what are called perfect and imperfect forms. The perfect form refers to completed action; the imperfect form is for actions not yet completed. Even in Modern Hebrew, which does have future, present, and past tenses, the verb "to be" (*hay-vav-hay*) does not have a present tense form, only a future and a past tense; we may say, "I was here," or "I will be here," but in the present tense we would simply say "I here"—the verb "to be" in its present tense (unlike the English "am" in "I am here") is implied. Since Moses is asking about what name to use at some future time, the response uses the imperfect verb form of the verb "to be," referring to an incomplete action. It could also be more simply translated as "I will be that which I will be." This translation seems to imply a difference between the now and the future and that because of this difference there really is no answer possible. Perhaps this response, couched in the grammatical form of an action not yet completed, is an indication that at some future point in time, linked to the liberation from oppression, God will simply be that which is.

In any case, it seems clear to me that no answer to the question of a name is given in this text. God's declining to answer the name question reveals a profound truth. No name or label could ever capture the true nature of the Divine. "I am" refers back to nothing less than the Nature of Being itself. We can say that "I am" is self-referential because any naming or outside labeling would presuppose an external point of view and hence a dualistic approach. This is precisely the depth of the divine revelation to Moses: that God is the Undivided Nature of Being, God is everything that is. When Moses reaches the children of Israel, he is to tell them that he has come because of the nature of things; in other words, what made him come to them is the truth of what is and what he now has realized. And this truth is that this way of people treating people (their enslavement) is a gross distortion of the true nature of Being. This truth ensures that oppressive systems based on ignorance will eventually cease to be.

Moses has recognized the affliction of his people, and whenever one looks clearly at the suffering of the world, it is simply the nature of Being to try to alleviate that suffering. Sometimes it is difficult to look clearly at suffering and oppression, but if we face the burning bush (that is, this life), it is our nature to be moved and to respond in some way. So we don't really need a name or even a leader to find liberation. Acting in accordance with our deepest nature and with the Truth of Being will show us the way.

The profound truth that God has no name is a hidden revelation of the Torah that even today is only slowly seeping into human consciousness. Moses himself seems not to have understood the response he received, and neither do the tellers of the narrative. In Exodus 3:15, God continues, "Thus shall you say to the children of Israel: YHVH, the God of Abraham, the God of Isaac, the God of Jacob, has sent me to you; this is my name forever." The emphasis here is on the instruction to Moses about what to "say." Also, how Moses will convey his experience is different from what was conveyed to him. The experience of the revelation was limited by the nature of Moses's own conceptualizing mind and by the limitations of his own beliefs and views. God must have a name if Moses is going to speak to the people, and so this verse is merely a reflection of what Moses would say.

The *aleph* of *ehyeh*, with the speaker (the Divine) referring to Itself, uses the first person imperfect form, which happens to be the same for masculine and feminine. This makes sense, since from the perspective of the non-dual, divine speech would not refer to its own manifestations—which are yet to come (imperfect form)—as either male or female.

The people (including Moses) will expect a name, and the verb "to be" is the basis for what he must say, but how do you put "Being" into language? *Ehyeh* refers to the divine nature of Being Unfolding. *YHVH*, by contrast, is what Moses is going to *say* to the people— "YHVH, the God of Abraham, the God of Isaac, the God of Jacob, has sent me to you; this is my name forever." What a difference between "I will be what I will be" and "YHVH—this is my name forever"! Moses expected to hear a name, so that is what he heard.

Since the time that this narrative originated, *Ehyeh asher Ehyeh* and *YHVH* have traditionally been understood, starting with Moses, as the answers to the request for a name, and they have de facto become names in how they generally are used. Traditional Jews call God *Hashem*, which is Hebrew for "the name." This misunderstanding reminds me of an event that happened with my daughter Esther when she was a young child. When Esther was three years old, my partner and I gave her a stuffed koala bear. I sat down with her on her bed and said, "Let's think of a name for the bear!" So we both started thinking, and when I had an idea, I started saying, "It could be …" but before I finished my sentence, she called out "Kibby?" She mistakenly heard me say "could be" as "Kibby," since she was already looking for a name. Kibby, of course, became the name of the koala bear, and Esther still has Kibby today (twenty-five years later). I think this is exactly what happened in the story with Moses: Moses hears the word *ehyeh* and thinks it is a name, *Ehyeh*.

What makes this passage so meaningful and important, I believe, is that despite the misunderstanding, it captures a profound revelatory moment that opens up an altogether new way of understanding the Divine. The intuitive insight captured by the text is that the Divine cannot adequately be understood through some image or concept or name, but rather we are meant to recognize that God is everything that is, the nature of Being itself. (Of course, "being itself" is a concept too, but at least it's pointing in the right direction.) Following the expulsion from the garden, human history was propelled by a sense of separation and duality imposed on the world through conceptual thinking (signified by the letter *bet*, the number two, that starts the book of Genesis). In Egypt, this development reaches its nadir, but here is also where the *aleph* process begins: the first letter of the word *ehyeh*—being an *aleph*—signifies the number one; it represents the non-dual. Where Genesis, which begins with a *bet*, is story of separateness and its consequences, here we find a way to begin reclaiming the oneness of all that is. Everything that comes into being is a part of the singular flow, the Unfolding of Being, or "Being Unfolding." I am that I am.

I believe that the metaphor of the burning bush can be seen as an early hint that we should change the way we relate to language. We need to free ourselves from the linguistic limitations of a God concept and a name for the Divine. Instead, we are invited to open up to the Ever-changing Flow of Being. Of course, we are not being asked to drop language altogether, or even the use of names; rather, we need to cultivate a new relationship to language and names by being aware of their all-pervasive influence on our perceptions of reality. We all have the ability to see directly and to observe the filtering effect of the language process and its influence on our minds. This is one of the potential benefits of contemplative practice and meditation.

7

Saying "You" to God

This book has been exploring the possibility of healing the rifts that have become such a pervasive and destructive force in our lives. These rifts alienate us from our own experience, from our bodies, from other people—even those closest to us—and from the planet; they essentially alienate us from "Everything There Is," or, as we may also say, from God. These rifts have been linked to conceptual thinking and its impact on the human mind. In order to free ourselves from the constraints of conceptual thinking, we have proposed a mystic path that emphasizes direct experience. Instead of *conceptualizing* the Divine Presence, analyzing it, or talking about it, we rather strive to *experience* it moment by moment in our lives. Any moment we open our hearts to the Divine Presence, any moment we experience it, we cultivate a loving relationship to All That Is. If this book has one lesson to offer, it is this: what we need to do is strive to overcome the sense of separation through clear seeing of its ultimately illusory nature. Once we have done that, there is nothing left but love.

A few years ago I was scheduled to lead a retreat with Sheila Peltz-Weinberg and Sylvia Boorstein. The retreat consisted mostly of silent, contemplative practice, but each day one of the teachers would also give a presentation. Sheila suggested that we coordinate our teachings around a particular theme, the second line of Psalm 65, "To You, silence is praise" (*Lecha dumiyah tehillah*), which is often cited as a Jewish proof text for the practice of silence. "Why doesn't each of us take one of the three words for our topic?" she asked. She suggested that Sylvia could cover praise, Sheila would talk about silence, and I would talk about God. Of course, Sheila knows me well, and so she had correctly assumed which of the topics I would want. But on this particular occasion, I had a slightly different idea. I was fine with the assignment, but I didn't want to talk *about* God; I rather wanted to discuss the topic of talking *to* God.

In this chapter I hope to explore what it means to be talking to God. By that I don't mean the traditional forms of Jewish prayer where one addresses God with words (though that could be a natural starting point). Instead, to me, "talking to God" is not a matter of using words at all. In fact, as we will see later, it is much closer to silently listening than to talking. It is not about using words, concepts, or ideas. Addressing God, saying "You" to God, to Everything There Is, is rather a state of heart and mind. It is a shift that occurs in our hearts and minds, a shift we experience as falling in love. To understand this, we need to reconceptualize what it means to say the word "You" and to describe what our experience is when there is a "You" present (whether or not the word "You" is vocalized).

Who Are You Talking to in Prayer?

Let's start our exploration by pointing to what makes this shift so difficult. My friend David Tapper *z"l* (may his memory be a blessing) was a big supporter of the Jewish renewal work I was involved with. He was also a longtime meditator, having learned Transcendental Meditation in the 1970s. Before I developed a contemplative practice on my own, he would regularly urge me to take up meditation. The Jewish renewal movement needs it, he would tell me over and over. Of course, he was thrilled to see this finally becoming a reality in the 1990s, when more and more rabbis were introduced to mindfulness and many synagogues began offering regular meditation groups. I know David would be pleased to see how far it has come today.

David considered himself a radical non-dualist, and as such he had problems with the idea of saying the word "You" in prayers. For example, the basic blessing formula of Judaism, which begins, *Baruch atah Adonay* [YHVH] *Elohaynu Melech ha-olam*, "Blessed are You, Lord [YHVH] our God, King of the world," simply baffled him: "Who are you talking to?" he would object. He felt that saying "You" to God implies seeing God as the other, as being a different and separate entity. In the normal use of language, you are you, and I am me, and the two seem to be separate entities. But, as this book has emphasized, this is a misunderstanding of the true nature of God.

Oddly enough, the words "blessed are You" when used in traditional prayer are often not spoken as an actual address to the Divine but rather pronounced as a fulfillment of an obligation to recite a formulaic liturgy without really saying "You" to God. One's belief or disbelief in the Divine is not at issue here; there is no such obligation in traditional prayer, since belief cannot be legislated. What can be made obligatory is the fulfilling of the recitation of particular language. By praying, observant Jewish atheists can fulfill their religious obligation without necessarily addressing the Divine. Likewise, believers in God need not feel they are actually addressing God at the moment of prayer to fulfill their obligation. However, in our context here, I am more interested in what it is like to actually address the Divine.

David's objection to the language of dualism is that it supports the illusion of separation. Yet, if we drop the language of kingship as the prime metaphor for the Divine, does this solve the problem? Or do we also need to drop praying "to" God as well? I think some insight lies in a Zen koan that, ironically, David himself introduced me to. (A koan is a statement that presents a paradox that puzzles the rational conceptual mind.) The koan is "Not one, not two." Like other Zen koans, this teaching does not allow for a simple resting in concepts.

It points out that even a profound concept like David's radical non-dualism is insufficient to express the whole picture of life. "Not one, not two." Life is not monistic, not dualistic. In response to David's objection over the use of the word "You," I pointed him to Martin Buber's teaching. Buber was a twentieth-century philosopher and scholar of Jewish mysticism. One of his major works, *I and Thou*, offers an analysis of the nature of separation or subject/object dualism as the perspective through which we see our everyday lives. Buber describes the experience of transcending this separation from a theological perspective. Let's take a look.

I and Thou

As a scholar of Jewish mysticism, Buber was influenced by many of the same teachings that I present in this book. His use of the concept or word "and" in the title of his book, *I and Thou*, for example, seems to be a direct outgrowth of the Jewish mystic's exploration of the Hebrew letter *vav* as it appears in the four letters of Divine Unfolding (*Yud Hay Vav Hay*). Remember that *vav* is in itself the Hebrew word for "and" as well as the word for "hook." In the book *I and Thou*, it is the *vav* that is the hook between the subject and object, the linking function that puts them in a relationship.

One of the central aspects of Buber's teaching in *I and Thou* is captured in the expression "I-It"; Buber calls "I-It" a primary word—a label I didn't fully understand until I began my own exploration of language's effect on experience. Buber believes that our moment-to-moment experience of life is filtered through conceptual language and that we perceive the world through the form of an "I-It" experience. We normally experience the world from the position of being the subject (me) of our own lives; the subject of my life, I, is having various experiences of worldly objects. I imagine you experience yourself as the subject of your experiences.

This subject, however, is not a thing in and of itself but a product of language; before language, there was no sense of a separate self having an experience. The "I" is the label given to this subject, and the various experiences are perceived as objects of experience and are referred to as "it." If I experience a color, I experience "it." If I hear a sound, I hear "it." If I have a thought, I think "it." "I" is the subject, and "it" is the object. Both exist only in relation to each other; without "I" there is no "it" and vice versa.

By referring to our basic experience of life on a moment-to-moment basis as an experience of the primary word "I-It," Buber was clearly indicating his sense that language is playing a critical role here. We are constantly saying or using the primary word "I-It"—whether we are speaking or not—because the mind uses this linguistic format to frame our experience of the world. We can say that "I-It" is the conceptual lens through which we usually perceive reality.

According to Buber, it is this "I-It" structure or lens that leads us to experience the world as one of alienation, isolation, and separation. The sense of existence in which we are separated from everything that is not "me" is an aspect of the world of *Assiyah/nefesh* in the four worlds model. Here, everything unfolds in a strict cause-and-effect relationship (hence the phrase "it is perfect"); it is the world of conditioned/conditional reality.

The consequences of this kind of framing have been discussed as the basic reactive patterns of the small mind. Simply put, when the "it" that is experienced is unpleasant, the mind manufactures volitional fabrications in the service of avoiding the experience; if it's pleasant, the mind manufactures thoughts designed to prolong or repeat the experience. Experiences that are neither pleasant nor unpleasant result in ignoring "it." Inasmuch as this thinking is a reactive manifestation that naturally occurs as a result of the "I-It" lens, it can be described as self-involved, self-serving, and self-centered.

But there is another primary word. As Buber says, "The attitude of a man is twofold, in accordance with the twofold nature of the [two] primary words which he speaks."[1] This other primary word is "I-Thou," and it transcends the separation of "I-It." Buber continues, "For the 'I' of the primary word 'I-Thou' is a different I from that of the primary word 'I-It.'"[2] The "I-Thou" experience is a state in which the subjective "I" disappears. This happens when the "and" manifests (thus the title of his book *I and Thou*), and the subject and object are no longer experienced separately as discrete "things." The "I-Thou" is hence a manifestation of the underlying connection referred to by the word "and."

It is worth noting that the English translation of the book's title needs some explanation. In the German original, the title is *Ich und Du—Ich* meaning "I," *und* meaning "and." The word that requires some explanation is *Du.* German has two renditions of what's conveyed by the English word "you": *du* and *Sie. Sie* is used in a formal sense of the English word "you," for example, when addressing someone you don't know, somebody of authority, and so on. *Du,* in contrast, indicates familiarity and intimacy. It's what is used within families and among friends. ("You are my friend" translates into *"Du bist mein Freund"*; by contrast, if we want to say, "Welcome to my home," to a stranger, Germans may say, *"Seien Sie willkommen in meinem Haus."*) This distinction doesn't exist in English, so in order to call attention to this specific usage of the German term, the English translators chose the word "thou." While that intent is certainly laudable, its functioning falls somewhat short. Generally, "thou" is not only rather anachronistic in English, but it also sounds rather formal to our ears; we would hardly speak to a beloved as "thou." The translation is hence misleading, and it's good to keep in mind that what is meant is to convey a sense of intimacy.

What is it that changes the relationship between subject and object? If we look at the letter *vav,* the Hebrew word for "and," we can gain some understanding. As mentioned earlier, *vav* is also the Hebrew word for "hook." The function of a hook, generally speaking, is to link together separate objects. Once these objects are linked or hooked, they are no longer completely separate entities, but they are now in relationship with each other. Imagine a fish caught on a hook. The fish can be seen as pulled toward the fisherman, but at the same time the fisherman is pulled by the fish. The muscles in the fisherman's arm behave differently based on the actions of the fish as well as his own intentions.

The *vav* or *das Zwischen* in German or the "and" in English is one of the four realms of the Unfolding of Divine Being, as discussed above. It is the world called *Yetzirah* and referred to by the soul/consciousness word *ruach*. Buber was a scholar of Jewish mysticism, and as such he must have been aware of this divine nature of this letter/word/concept. I believe he conceived it not merely or only as representing one aspect of the Divine, but in fact as *the* aspect of the Divine that has the power to overcome the separation caused by the conceptualizing mind, the mind that divides the world into "I" and "it."

Remarkably, in biblical Hebrew the letter *vav* has a double linguistic function. As described above, it can mean "and"; if used this way, it's called the *vav hachibur*, "the conjunctive *vav*." But it can also be used as a *vav hahipuch*, "the *vav* of reversal"; in this function, it reverses the tense of the verb that follows. Remember that biblical Hebrew does not use the three tenses of past, present, and future. Instead there are only two tenses called perfect and imperfect—the perfect tense referring to a completed action, the imperfect to one that's not yet completed. Now, if the verb following the *vav hahipuch* is in the perfect tense, this *vav* changes its meaning to the imperfect. For example, a well-known verse from Exodus says, "And you shall love YHVH with all your heart" (Deuteronomy 6:5). The Hebrew transliteration is *V'ahavta et YHVH Elohecha b'chol l'vavcha*. The first word of this phrase, *v'ahavta*, starts with a *vav* appended to the word *ahavta*. That word, *ahavta*, is in the perfect tense and means "you loved." With the added *vav hahipuch*, however, the word means "you will love," which is the imperfect tense. In Genesis 1:3, we read the word *vayomer*. *Yomer* is imperfect and means "He [God] will speak"; when the *vav hahipuch* is appended, however, it becomes the perfect tense, "He [God] spoke." Linguistically, this is a fascinating phenomenon, as it points to the transformative nature of the word *vav*. It's as if the language itself were capturing the transformative power of connection. When the *vav*, "and," manifests, there is a reversal from a sense of separateness from an object (it) to a sense of connection to that object (i.e., it is You), to an experience of relationship.

In this sense, the meaning of *vav* goes far beyond its linguistic functions. Earlier, we looked at Jacob's story in Genesis where he was wrestling with an angel. I suggested that Jacob was rather "wrestling" with his inner demons—his ego-need to receive the blessing of the firstborn, his willingness to be a deceiver, and so forth. But once Jacob is ready to face those qualities and pay attention (Loving Attention) rather than running away from them, once he embraces his inner demons, he is transformed into an angel. This paying attention is a manifestation of the *vav*, and as a result of this connecting, he is no longer who he was before.

So by understanding the *vav*, "and," now we are in a better position to ask what Buber means when he refers to the shifting from "I-It" to "I-Thou" as the primary word.

> When *Thou* is spoken, the speaker has no thing for his object. For where there is a thing there is another thing. Every *It* is bounded by others; *It* exists only through being bounded by others. But when *Thou* is spoken, there is no thing. *Thou* has no bounds.
>
> When *Thou* is spoken, the speaker has no *thing*; he has indeed nothing. But he takes his stand in relation.[3]

The fundamental shift described here is one in which the boundaries disappear in recognition of the joint existence of what formerly was experienced as subject and object. In moments of "I-Thou," there is the recognition/realization of the nature of inter-being. Mental objects continue to arise and continue to be experienced, but they are arising and continuing within the context of the relationship. Everything that is being experienced is in fact codetermined by prior causes and conditions. However, without the connection, the *vav*/"and" that can manifest through Loving Attention, they are not part of a "between" but part of the I-It causes.

Here is a small example that reflects this shift. When I lead a retreat and try to explain this teaching to a group of listeners, my experience usually begins from an "I-It" position. I want to accomplish something. I have material to present and an objective in mind. My intention may be wholesome, but mixed in there often is also a self-serving need for being liked, appreciated, understood, and loved. Then I start presenting, and in the process of addressing my audience, something may begin to shift. If and as I am able to be somewhat cognizant to my audience, I can sense their experience moment by moment. Initially, I may just notice someone smile or nod, but as a result I begin to adjust my talk, emphasizing some points, dropping others, changing my tone, and so on. I deviate from my initial presentation plan (the "It" of my prepared notes) in favor of a dancelike interaction between the audience and me. The boundaries between speaker and listeners have begun to soften, and I start recognizing that my experience isn't just "mine" but rather a product of the interaction between me and the group. I may begin to see the "Thou" in various listeners. Slowly, parts of the teaching shift into a shared experience of "I and Thou."

Buber called this a "relational moment," a phrase I very much appreciate. There still is a "You" and an "I" in the experience, but they are not separate; the "I" exists only in relationship to the "Thou" and is thus no longer the "I" as in "I-It." There is an objective world, a world filled with objects, but the "I"s experiencing this world are different depending on how deeply they recognize the nature of their relationship with the objects in the world. For Buber, the shift from "I-It" to "I-Thou" is a spiritual experience that underlies what he refers to as the "eternal Thou."

In my own use of the four worlds model, the objective world "I-It" is in fact one form of manifestation of Divine Unfolding; "It" (the world) is an aspect of that Unfolding. The "I-It" consciousness, however, is unable to recognize the divinity of the world. It is, in essence, ignorant of its true nature and of its relationship to it. Wisdom about the actual nature of "worldly" objects is brought about only through Loving Attention, the connective force (represented in the *vav*) through which the "I-Thou" consciousness arises and is able to recognize its own underlying interconnected nature.

Be Careful Talking about God

For Buber, "God" is not something we should discuss or analyze through language, since all the talk about God's Being and God's work is mostly a misunderstanding derived from the "I-It" consciousness. While I understand Buber's skepticism, I believe that it could be worth reclaiming the word "God" if it can serve as a springboard into the practice of relational awareness. In my praying practice, I try to move beyond language about God, yet I often find the God language helpful if it is used as a reminder to directly experience the interconnectivity of all there is. (Language can also be a convenient shorthand to describe a relational moment after it has passed.) Buber himself concedes an understanding of "God" that avoids the traditional trappings:

> For he who speaks the word God and really has *Thou* in mind
> ... addresses the true *Thou* of his life, which cannot be limited
> by another *Thou*, and to which he stands in a relation that gathers up and includes all others. But when he, too, who abhors the
> name, and believes himself to be godless, gives his whole being to
> addressing the *Thou* of his life, as a *Thou* that cannot be limited
> by another, he addresses God.[4]

Really saying "You" to God is not a verbal act at all. It is a change in consciousness and perception in a moment of awakened experience. In discussing the I and Thou experience, Buber says:

> It does not use speech, yet begets it. We perceive no *Thou*, but none the less we feel we are addressed and we answer—forming, thinking, acting. We speak the primary word [I-Thou] with our being, though we cannot utter *Thou* with our lips.[5]

The psalmist says, "Yea, though I walk through the valley of the shadow of death, I will fear no evil, for Thou art with me" (Psalm 23:4). What the psalmist is describing here is an experience of Presence in the midst of a life-threatening moment. Whatever he was facing, he did not feel alone or separate or deserted. In moments of fear or confusion, our "I-It" lens may easily lead us to see the world in terms self-preservation or blame or revenge. But through training in practicing Loving Attention, it is possible to recognize the fear itself as another "You," as another part of our heart/mind. By calling it "You," we are not separating the particulars of this "You" experience from any other aspect of "You." Paraphrasing the words of the Baal Shem Tov, "Everything is 'You' and nothing but 'You.'" The original teaching of "everything is God and nothing but God" is a conceptual teaching. "Everything is 'You' and nothing but 'You'" describes the experience of the non-dual. But even that phrase is more of a retrospective summary of the actual experience; when we pay Loving Attention, we greet everything that is arising with, "Oh, it's you."

Saying "You" to God Is Not Speech but a Change in Consciousness

To really say "You" is not a function of speech but rather a presenting of our entire being to the present moment. It opens us to the truth of what is, recognizing the interconnectedness of all phenomena. It is selfless because the "I" (of "I-It") is no longer experiencing itself as a separate entity. It gives birth to an "I" (the "I" of "I-Thou") that is always latent but not always manifest. Through the process of Loving Attention to what is arising, wisdom and understanding manifest, and thoughts of loving-kindness and compassion proliferate, ultimately leading to wholesome actions in the world. The experience of "You and I" manifests as "I Love You," and the word "Love" is just another form of the word "and."

Buber would say that the "I-Thou" experience arises in a moment of grace and cannot be manufactured. It is true that as long as we strive for something to happen, we are propelled by the "I-It" mode of thinking; the desired experience, here the "I-Thou" moment, is just another separate object to be attained. But we can foster the conditions in which these moments of grace are more likely to become manifest. In particular, the practice of Loving Attention to the unfolding of each moment will allow us to deeply see the truth of interconnection as the fundamental reality of life. Seeing this reality is the realization of "I and Thou." In a way we can say that these moments of grace don't need to be manufactured because they already are present—just obscured by "I-It" ideation. Here lies a great paradox of our practice: we experience a different reality only by accepting things just the way they are in this moment and in this reality.

The *Dudele* of Reb Levi Yitzhak

One approach to addressing the Divine was offered by Levi Yitzchak of Berditchev, a Hasidic rebbe in the second generation of followers of the Baal Shem Tov. He offered his theology in the form of a song, known as a *dudele* (from the Yiddish word *du* for "you"). Levi Yitzchak presents us a way of looking at the world through the eyes of the teaching "Everything is God and nothing but God." And in doing so, he personalizes the experience of mindfulness.

The *dudele* is originally written in Yiddish; the translation below is mine. It stays close to the text, except for the beginning and the end. The opening address to God, *Riboyno shel oylom*, literally means "Master of the world," but I replaced it with the metaphor I have been using in this book. I also added the last three stanzas to include formal mindfulness practice experiences. A recorded version of the *dudele* can be found at www.awakenedheartproject.org.[6]

The Dudele of Levi Yitzchak of Berditchev

Riboyno shel oylom (3x)
Ich vil dir a dudele zingen:
Du du du du du

Holy Being of the World (3x)
I want to sing a *dudele* for You
Du du du du, You You You You

Where shall I seek You?
And where shall I not seek You?
Where can I find You?
And where can I not find You?
Du du du du, You You You You

If I go, You, if I stay, You
Only You, always You
Here You, there You
Du du du du, You You You You

Az iz gut, du,
choliloh shlect oich, du
When it's good, You
Forfend sorrow, You
Du du du du, You You You You

Tingle You, pressure You
Warm You, cold You
Du du du du, You You You You

Judgment You, *Hesed* You
Pleasant You, unpleasant You
Du du du du, You You You You

Walking You, sitting You
Standing You, eating You
Du du du du, You You You You

Praise You, blame You
Fame You, ill repute You
Du du du du, You You You You

Reb Levi Yitzchak is singing a love song to God. It's easy to feel how personal his words are compared to a standard blessing form like "We bless You YHVH, King of the universe." He is filled with the love for God; he experiences God in whatever appears to him, wherever he goes. In our own practice, we can develop that same love, and we can start by singing a love song to ourselves, to our own experiences, and then widen it to all beings and to the Holy One of Being. I believe this is the sentiment of the core Jewish teachings *V'ahavta l'rayacha kamocha*, "You shall love your neighbor as you love yourself" (Leviticus 19:18) and *V'ahavta et YHVH Elohecha*, "You shall love YHVH your God" (Deuteronomy 11:1). We all can cultivate the capacity of saying "I love You" to this entire Divine Unfolding of Being that we and the world are. Our silent Loving Attention is one giant prayer of praise.

Saying "You" to God is not an act of speech; in fact, it's not something to "do" at all. Rather, it's a presenting of our whole being to the present moment. It is more a listening than a speaking. In order for me to say "You" to God, I need to pay attention. *Shema Yisrael YHVH Elohaynu YHVH echad*, one of the central lines of Jewish prayer, is a practice instruction where we remind ourselves to pay attention (*shema* is the imperative form of "to listen"). We need to listen from that place where we are connected to our inner experience (*Yisrael*), to YHVH, the Unfolding of Being. That is our God (*Elohaynu*); there is no more subject/object duality (I-It). YHVH is not an "It" but the "Thou," and "Thou" is not an object separate from other objects but All One Unfolding. As relational beings we experience "Thou" as "I and Thou," or as You and I. I am not separate from You, and You are not separate from that which I am.

In my experience, there is another primary word that expresses reality beyond "me," beyond the experience of a separate self. That primary word is "I Am." "I Am" is not other than the "Total Unfolding of Being." It is alluded to in YHVH or in that little word "God."

Part IV

The Awakened Heart and the End of Separation

8

Living with an Awakened Heart

Ain't you got a right to the tree of life?
OLD SPIRITUAL SONG

Ayekah? [Where did you go?]
GENESIS 3:9

Love is the true nature of the Divine Unfolding of Being. It is that Unfolding of Being which is "I Am." You are that as well. Our love for each other is who we are when we are not scared and confused and cut off and shut down. This is the message that I hope you will take away from our exploration.

The Communal Revelation at Sinai

Let me pull together a few strands that have woven their way through this narrative. Early in this book I said that my spiritual journey was propelled by the question "Who am I?" As my contemplative practice matured and deepened, I began to recognize the power of language, and over the years that question grew to include "What am I?" and "How am I?" What I discovered is that most of what I identify as "I" or "me" or "mine" are simply conceptual labels and that these labels form something like a patina on the true nature of this life. But there is also something that remained, a sense of "I Am" that is clearly not me. It is what knows me.

In Deuteronomy 5:5, Moses addresses the people in one of his final discourses, saying, *Anochi omed bayn YHVH u'vaynaychem ba-ayt ha-hee*, "I stood between YHVH and you at that time"—Moses is referring to the time of the revelation at Sinai when all the children of Israel were there, and they received what are usually called the ten commandments. The common explanation of the events that transpired at the time of this revelation is that somewhere in the middle of that revelatory process, the people drew away from the mountain and told Moses to go get the revelation for them. In this verse, Moses is reminding them of that time.

The Baal Shem Tov, however, gives us a very different interpretation. The deeper meaning here, he says, is that rather than *anochi* referring to Moses in this sentence, *anochi* is referring to the sense each person has of "I Am" that stands between you and God. I am very moved by this teaching. There are at least two ways we can understand this message: if something stands between you and God, it might be seen as something that's in your way of getting to God; or it is something that's a gateway for getting to God. I believe if we think of the "I Am" as referring to a separate self, to something that's me and mine, then we only create a barrier to realizing the true nature of the Divine; it is the result of the *bet* story of Genesis, a product of dualistic thinking. However, the Torah has two *aleph* stories that serve to heal that dualistic rift. We have already explored the first one in the word *Ehyeh* (a word that begins with the letter *aleph*) that came to Moses at the burning bush. Let's take a look at the other *aleph* experience—the one that takes place at Sinai.

In the revelation of the ten "commandments," the first commandment uses these words: *Anochi YHVH Elohecha asher hotzaytee-cha may-eretz mitzrayim mi-bayt avadim*. This might be traditionally translated as "I am the Lord thy God, who brought thee out of the land of Egypt, out of the house of bondage" (Exodus 20:2). However, I believe this could be read as *Anochi YHVH*, followed by a period, meaning "I am YHVH." "I Am" is nothing other than *Yud Hay Vav Hay*; the "I Am" is the YHVH experience. The experience that each of us is the YHVH process is the recognition that YHVH is *Elohecha* (your God). It Is You and You Are It. The recognition of that reality is what liberates you from the narrow place of Egypt, the place of bondage (the illusion of separateness that leads humans to act so selfishly as to create slavery).

The word *Anochi* also begins with the Hebrew letter *aleph*. The difference between the two *aleph* stories is profound. While the *aleph* of *Ehyeh* was revealed only to Moses, the *aleph* of *Anochi* was given to all people at Sinai (as the first letter of the ten commandments); the revelation is communal. Since *aleph* is a silent letter, this refers to a revelation beyond words and concepts. What it tells us is that we all are the singular Unfolding of Being. That is the deeper truth behind the letters *YHVH*.

The Tree of Life—Oneness as Love

We often think of oneness as the opposite of multiplicity, but that only shows a limit of our conceptual thinking. Oneness is actually all-inclusive. It brings everything into a single embrace; it includes everything, and that is why it is the same as love.

This understanding is beautifully illustrated by a metaphor that is central to all of Judaism: the Tree of Life. In normative Judaism, the Torah is referred to as a Tree of Life. And in mystical Judaism, this tree is placed at the heart of a mystical system referred to as the ten *sefirot* (emanations), which illustrates how divine energy is transformed into the form of a world.

The image is so powerful because it captures the primordial nature of the force that shapes the Unfolding of Being; it captures the force that shapes who/what/how we truly are. It is a symbol for the Jewish mystical understanding of the task of human life: to heal the rift that causes us to perceive the world in terms of duality. The separation of heaven (*shamayim*) and earth (*aretz*) is mentioned in the first line of the Torah (Genesis 1:1). The image of the Tree of Life is one of a connection between heaven and earth, a constant channel that allows energy to flow naturally, in both directions, from place to place. That connection is love. And because love is not some external entity, but the very essence of our own nature, we can reclaim it as our birthright.

When the Jewish mystics created the symbolic system called the ten *sefirot* depicting the flow of divine energy, they placed the Tree of Life in the very center of that system. Whether we call the Tree of Life *Tiferet* (Compassion), one of the ten *sefirot*; or the *Vav* (And) of the Hebrew *Yud Hay Vav Hay*; or the *Ruach* of the worlds *Nefesh, Ruach, Neshamah*—ultimately, it all boils down to the same teaching, the teaching of love.

In mystical practice there is a deep experiencing of love as the central aspect of life, a straight equivalent to what life actually is. And that Love is the binding or connecting force that shapes and unifies All Being.

Everything That Comes into Being wants to be connected (through Love) to Everything Else in Being, since the Connecting Force is an aspect of All Being. As my teacher Reb Zalman once said, even gravity is a form of love: love on the physical plain.

Using Numerology to Point to the Oneness of Life, Love, and Language

As we approach the end of our exploration into some of the challenging aspects of human existence, I would like to share a different way of looking at what has been discussed. Jewish mystics make extensive use of numerology, which I initially understood to be a kind of mathematical proof of various assertions. But I came to realize that it can also be regarded as a way of introducing us to new ways of seeing, a way that breaks the molds of our conventional categories and softens the rigidity of conceptual thinking. The point need not always be seen as proving something to the rationalizing conceptual mind; rather, it asserts underlying connections in life that we may not have noticed. It can be a tool for keeping revelation alive.

Jewish mystics were highly creative in superimposing their deep experience of unity and love into the words of Torah. They were particularly drawn to a verse from Zechariah: "On that day YHVH will be one and God's name will be one" (14:9). To them, this verse alludes to a future life beyond separation and beyond duality. The mystics understood that as long as we think of God as something with a name, we are not in the place of oneness. So they deconstructed the linguistic sense of YHVH as a concept and instead used it as a metaphor for a pathway that reveals the direction we must take to find that unity.

The name *Yud Hay Vav Hay*, they point out, has a numerical value of 26. (The number is derived from the position of the four letters in the Hebrew alphabet: *Yud* is the tenth letter, *Hay* the fifth, and *Vav* the sixth; hence, $10 + 5 + 6 + 5 = 26$.) To the mystics, this number is still associated with seeing God from a dualistic perspective. It represents the nature of Moses's relation to YHVH *before* Moses had his most profound realization of the Divine.

Exodus 33:11 then tells us the story of Moses experiencing this profound realization: "And YHVH would speak to Moshe face to face, as a man speaks to his neighbor." Yet Moses was not satisfied with that level of relationship and asks for more. So, he is instructed to climb up Mount Sinai once again, and this time God passes before him. It is then that Moses is granted the even deeper realization of seeing the world through God's eyes.[1] With this view, we no longer look at the Divine as something outside of ourselves; we are no longer face-to-face, but rather aligned with "God's face" from the inside. Now there is only one face. We are now seeing the world through

God's eyes. From this perspective, Moses is told that YHVH's name will be called out—a hint that YHVH's name is not YHVH.

> [19] He said:
>   I myself will cause all my Goodliness to pass
>   in front of your face,
>   I will call out the name of YHVH
>   before your face:
>   that I show-favor to whom I show-favor,
>   that I show-mercy to whom I show-mercy.
> [20] But he said:
>   You cannot see my face,
>   for no human can see me and live!
>   EXODUS 33:19–20

The Torah says that when Moses has this peak experience, the name of YHVH that gets called out is *"Yud Hay Vav Hay;* Compassion and Tenderness, Patience, Forbearance, Kindness, Awareness; Bearing love from age to age; lifting guilt and mistakes and making us free" (Exodus 34:6–7).[2] This is what the early Rabbis refer to as the thirteen-fold name of God. As is the case with the revelation at the burning bush, "I Will Be What I Will Be," this too is not a name as we usually think of names but rather a description of God's nature.

It's difficult to determine what exactly the thirteen names are, and later commentators propose various ways of combining the words to get to thirteen names. However, this misses the point that the Rabbis who first referred to it as "the thirteen-fold name" were making. They were editorializing on the centrality of this particular revelation in their theology. Exodus 33 might be seen as the ultimate or "peak" revelation of Torah. Each of the thirteen names points to a different "loving" aspect of the Divine, but underlying all of them is a oneness of love; together they are All That Is. Thirteen is a representation of oneness. And it is also a representation of love.

This numerological interpretation becomes even more apparent when we look at the Hebrew word for "one," *echad*. *Echad* consists of the Hebrew letters *aleph*, *chet*, and *dalet*. *Aleph* is the first letter, *chet* the eighth letter, and *dalet* the fourth letter: $1 + 8 + 4 = 13$.

As shown above, *YHVH* has the numerical value of twenty-six. That value is associated with Moses's (or our own) experience of seeing the Divine as something "out there," face-to-face. Half of twenty-six is thirteen—oneness, the non-dualistic nature of the Divine. The shift from Moses's first realization at the burning bush to this revelation represents the shift from duality to non-duality.

But the mystics don't stop there; they simultaneously make yet another point to emphasize the relationship among YHVH, *echad*, and love. The Hebrew word for "love" is *ahavah*, made up of the letters *aleph*, *hay*, *bet*, and *hay*. *Aleph* is the first letter, *hay* the fifth, *bet* the second. *Ahavah* has the numerical value $1 + 5 + 2 + 5 = 13$! *Ahavah* (love) has the same value as *echad* (one).

And as we have previously discussed, love (*ruach*) was what existed in the beginning; it was already present before anything was spoken into being. Human beings invented speech as a means of creating this world, or rather these worlds we live in. The first instance of "and God said" (*vayomer*) occurs in Genesis 1:3. What was there before this? *V'ruach Elohim m'rachefet al p'nay hamayim* (Genesis 1:2). "The *ruach* aspect of Divinity was hovering over the face [or at the interface] of what was as yet unformed" (my translation). This is the status even before the words "Let there be light" are spoken.

It is important to see that the "worlds" we humans spoke into being are not any less a manifestation of the Divine; their divine nature is simply hidden under the veils of separation that our conceptual thinking has woven. With the advent of speech came the sense of separation. A new "reality" map was created, and ever since we have lived in the "realities" we created. In a way, we can say that we began to inhabit the map rather than the actual reality we were mapping.

If we look at the biblical account, what is the first thing that happens after humans eat from the Tree of the Knowing of Good and Evil?

She took of its fruit and she ate and she gave also to her man beside her and he ate. And the eyes of them both were opened and they knew they were naked [i.e., became self-conscious]. They sewed fig leaves together and made themselves loincloths. And they heard the voice [*kol*] of YHVH Elohim walking about in the garden as *ruach* at that point of the day. And the human and his wife hid themselves from facing YHVH Elohim in the trees of the garden. And YHVH Elohim called out to the human and YHVH Elohim said to the human, "Where are you?" (Genesis 3:6–9).[3]

The voice of God is coming from the *ruach*, the heart aspect. "Where are you?" the heart calls out. This is what happens when we get cut off and lost in thought: the heart calls out to us, "Where did you go?" Whenever we are lost, we need to listen to that part of ourselves that is crying out, "Where are you?" You can practice realizing this experience through exercise 5 in the appendix.

Ending Separation and Living with an Awakened Heart

In this book, I have explored the sense of separation that pervades our lives and inflicts so much pain and suffering. I hope to have shown that it is possible to overcome this separation. We all can live from the place of an awakened heart! Awakening is nothing but the realization of what is our inherent nature: a true, loving, divine nature of heart/mind.

Right in the middle of the mystical prayer of the *Kabbalat Shabbat* (receiving the Sabbath) service, we hear, "Wake up, wake up. Your Light has already come." Awakening does not mandate us to change our essential nature. The love we are looking for is already what we are. That is the message of the Sabbath, the seventh day—we don't have to do or create something; we only need to awaken to what we are. Our *ruach*, our loving nature, preceded the confused states of thought that led to selfishness.

In biblical Hebrew the word *lev* means "heart/mind"; in Modern Hebrew it means only "heart." It is this separation of heart and mind that I have been addressing. According to the Zohar, when we left the Garden of Eden, speech went into exile (separation) from voice. Speech here represents the world of conceptual thinking, a world filled with beliefs, views, and opinions (including the view of a separate self); voice is a metaphor for the heart. Obviously, the work you are reading right now is also filled with words, beliefs, views, and opinions. But I hope it has become clear that my intention is not to simply present yet another belief system to adhere to. It is offered as something for you to reflect on in your practice of paying Loving Attention to the truth of your own experience as it is unfolding, present moment by present moment. The thinking, conceptualizing mind is a powerful tool that can be used wisely—as long as we understand its nature and its limitations by paying Loving Attention to it.

Through our practice we can cultivate an awareness that is both mindful and heartful. Among spiritual seekers we hear a lot about the power of mindfulness, and I think it is important that we begin to see (and call) it for what it also is: heartfulness.

A change in language—from "mindfulness" to "heartfulness"— carries with it implications for our practice beyond expanding our perspective in contemplation. We often think of the mind as something that's located somewhere in the region of our brain. But that is actually a misperception. It projects to a specific location a phenomenon that is not exactly located at any one point in space. I think this misperception is due to a rather common error: we confuse our thoughts with our mind. It may well be the case that our conceptual thoughts are primarily generated in the brain. It may also be that the sense doors for sight, hearing, smelling, and tasting are primarily located in the head region. Hence, much of the raw data that is processed by the mind is indeed generated in the region of the head. But that doesn't mean that the mind is limited to those functions.

I recently heard my teachers describe it like this: Think of a modern airplane. We know that it is possible to let the autopilot—a function of the computer—fly the plane for long stretches. But the computer is still not the pilot. Similarly, we could see our brain as the computer of the body. It serves an important function, but that doesn't make it the heart/mind.

Rather, if we live with the heart/mind as the "pilot," then we can fully utilize the information generated by the brain without having to switch to autopilot. We can live fully embodied and with a sense that the mind is just one function of the infinitively vaster heart/mind. Lately, I have been practicing heartful attention, moment by moment sensing and relating everything I notice to the heart area of my body; it is quite amazing how conducive the shift from the head to the heart is to cultivating Loving Attention.

In my practice I frequently aim at cultivating a heart of loving-kindness; I do this through the recitation of phrases of blessing that I silently repeat over and over:

> May I be blessed with peace.
> May I be blessed with joy.
> May I be blessed with loving-kindness.
> May I be blessed with compassion.

In this practice I regularly change the phrases such that I include all other beings—for example, "May all beings be blessed with peace."[4] When repeating these blessings in my heart/mind, I try to feel them being offered from the place of my physical heart, not from my head. Most of us are probably familiar with offering caring thoughts or words from the heart space. This same heart space can also be used not only for *offering* loving thoughts but also as the source of *taking in* each moment and noticing what is arising here and now. Try for yourself! In my experience, changing the locus of reception from the head to the heart has immediate positive consequences.

As we begin to pay attention from the place of the heart, the reactive patterns of our minds begin almost immediately to transform. When practicing mindfulness from the place of the head, I notice sensations arising and whether they are pleasant or unpleasant. This generally causes an immediate reaction in the discursive aspect of my mind: to strategize how to get rid of unpleasant sensations and hold on to pleasant ones. By contrast, when I shift to heartfulness, I notice that with the arising of an unpleasant sensation there comes an instant sense of compassion. Similarly, pleasant sensations lead to appreciation of the moment rather than to plans for holding on to it. The process might be described as a shift from thinking about what I am experiencing to tracking how I feel about what I am experiencing. I believe this shift is a natural consequence of moving beyond the separation of head from heart. In practice 2 in the appendix, you can begin to refocus your attention on the heart center.

When we recognize that what we are is Awareness (*Yud*) Connected through Loving Attention (*Vav*) to the Truth of Whatever Is Arising (*Hay*) Comprehended through Wisdom (*Hay*), we move beyond the alienation caused by the conceptualizing brain. We then see the world through the eyes of love. The unity of Exodus 33, "seeing the world through God's eyes," can also be expressed as God seeing the world through our eyes. This clear seeing and loving connection to what is seen impels us to act kindly to "Everything Unfolding in Being." This is the point of practice.

Acknowledgments

The teachings in this book are the result of the great fortune I have had to be influenced by some remarkable teachers. The ideas I am presenting come primarily from the intersection between the teachings of the Jewish mystics, the wisdom of the dharma (as presented by the teachers of mindfulness), and my direct experience in contemplative practice. But without these particular people in my life, my practice might never have occurred.

The Jewish spiritual practices that so move me were inspired by my connection to Reb Zalman Schachter-Shalomi *z"l*. From the first time I heard his teachings on audiocassette, I knew that his was a voice I needed to listen to. They were introduced to me by Rabbi Aryeh Hirschfield *z"l*. When, a year later, I met Reb Zalman in person, I was inspired enough to change my life path and attend rabbinical school in Philadelphia, where Reb Zalman lived. I had the good fortune to become his aide and travel around the world with him, listening to him teach people of all faiths. He modeled for me the value of integrating and synthesizing spiritual wisdom from any source of truth.

Reb Zalman was also the one who introduced me to Sylvia Boorstein, who then became my primary contemplative teacher. From our very first meeting, I realized that I wanted to be involved in teaching the same wisdom that she presented and modeled in her life. She took me on as a trainee in both practicing and teaching Jewish mindfulness meditation. Fortunately, Rabbi Sheila Peltz-Weinberg was part of the same group. Together we led about thirty retreats that were aimed at synthesizing mindfulness and Jewish spirituality. Sheila's teachings are inspirational, and together we are still working on training the next generation of teachers.

I am also greatly indebted to Rabbi David and Shoshana Cooper, with whom I taught dozens of retreats. They too were part of the original effort to synthesize the two traditions, and I had an opportunity to learn from the depth of their spiritual experience. Likewise, Norman Fischer and Rabbi Alan Lew *z"l* became teaching colleagues, and they too led to a deepening of my practice. Norman is still a close mentor for me in this practice.

Finally, I am strongly influenced by the teachings of Ajahn Sumedho. His clear teachings on resting in awareness have become central to my practice. Ajahn Sumedho also made me realize the tremendous power of language and conceptual thinking in shaping the human mind. Many of the core ideas in this book flowed out of practicing with his insights.

Brian Arnell is my colleague at the Awakened Heart Project. He has been present at the first formulation of many of the teachings in this book, and his appreciation as well as his comments give me continued energy to explore and present. He is one of my biggest supporters and the person who most helps set up the opportunities to teach.

All of my life efforts are supported by my soul mate, co-parent, teaching partner, and fellow traveler on life's journeys, Rabbi Joanna Katz. She has been an inspiration as a student and teacher of contemplative practice. She has listened to me present the ideas in this book in numerous settings, public and private, and has helped shape my thinking, especially in applying these teachings to daily life.

I am indebted to my friend and the editor of this book, Jurgen Mollers. He discussed, in great depth, every idea and word in this manuscript. He played a large role in organizing how to present the ideas. He urged me at every step to be clearer on my ideas. His enthusiasm for the material gave me confidence that it was worth presenting to you, the reader. What a blessing to have someone so willing to listen to my every formulation of the truth of my experience.

Thanks to all those at Jewish Lights who have believed in me enough to value and publish my work. As I write this acknowledgment, they are busy getting the book into final form, as well as already promoting it. I appreciate all their hard work.

Finally, I am grateful to my students. They are the real inspiration for this work. As I see how the practice is as helpful to them as it is to me, they give meaning to my life. I feel that we are on a spiritual quest together, and I hope to have many more years to practice with them.

Accompanying Contemplative Practices

Practice 1   YHVH Breathing

As we see throughout the book, the four letters *Yud Hay Vav Hay* serve as a springboard to exploring the nature of the Divine. One practice approach uses these letters in a contemplative way by linking them to the cycle of breath. Since the letter *hay* is the Hebrew equivalent of the English letter "h," it is naturally related to the sound of breath. The letter "h" is sounded by breathing out. The almost identical same sound occurs when we breathe in. From this perspective the four letters *Yud Hay Vav Hay* could be seen as containing within them an in-breath and an out-breath. *Yud* is the smallest letter in the Hebrew alphabet and has been considered by Jewish mystics as a placeholder for the nothingness before the "everything" that arises in conditioned reality. In the cycle of breath, it would represent the space at the end of each out-breath before the in-breath begins. At that moment, the lungs are in their least air-filled state and actually get smaller. Then comes an in-breath (*hay*), and the lungs go into their most full state. That full state can be linked to the letter *vav*. *Vav* is the straightest letter in the Hebrew alphabet. It is a straight line and can be thought of as a metaphoric equivalent to the spine. The spine is in its straightest form at the end of the in-breath. In this way the *vav* corresponds to fullness in the same way that the *yud* corresponds to emptiness. Finally, with another *hay* comes the out-breath, and the cycle repeats itself. As long as we are alive and breathing, we are constantly manifesting the *Yud Hay Vav Hay* with each breath.

Sit comfortably and begin to notice the bodily sensations of the breath coming in. Continue to notice what the bodily experience is of the ending of each in-breath and the sensations before the out-breath begins. Notice the sensations of the out-breath and the sensations as the out-breath ends before the next in-breath occurs. As a way of exaggerating the noticing you can see what it feels like to prolong any of the four stages. You can also practice noticing the sensations without any conscious effort to lengthen or shorten any of the four stages. As you notice each of the four stages, softly begin to add a mental label on top of (not instead of) the actual sensory experience. Before the in-breath begins you might label that experience with the Hebrew letter *yud*. As the breath comes in, softly label that experience as *hay*. At the end of the in-breath and before the out-breath, add the label *vav*. And with the out-breath, add the label *hay* again. This repeats with each breath.

This is a practice that can help us realize that YHVH is the process of life we are experiencing as long as we are alive. It can help us recognize the impermanent nature of any particular experience. One cannot continue breathing in indefinitely no matter how pleasant it is to take a breath. It can help us recognize the cyclical nature of Life Unfolding.

Try exchanging the labels of *yud, hay, vav,* and *hay* with the labels of "empty," "in," "full," and "out." This helps make the link between the letters and the process they represent. Keep in mind as well the following verse from Genesis 2:7:

> And YHVH, God, formed the human, of the dust from the soil,
> He blew into his nostrils the breath of life [*nishmat chayyim*]
> and the human became a living being [*nefesh chayah*].

This verse makes explicit the relationship between us as living human beings with YHVH God. Breath is how the two are inter-related. And with that first breath, one might ask whether it was an in-breath or an out-breath. It is obvious when asked in this way that the answer is a matter of perspective. From the earth perspective it is an in-breath. From the YHVH God perspective it is an out-breath. Same one breath. This is the nature of Inter-being. As humans we breathe in oxygen, the out-breath of the plant world. We breathe out carbon dioxide, the in-breath of the plant world. We "inter-are" with the beings of that realm.

Practice 2 Energy/Heart Breathing

In this practice it is possible to sensitize yourself to experiencing a flow of energy in the body that manifests as a sense of tingling or vibration. At first this may be visualization or imagining of experience. Eastern teachings about *chi* or energy posit that there is a flow of energy that follows the directing of attention to various parts of the body. As you become more attuned to your bodily experience, it is possible to actually feel energy flowing to/through parts of the body. It may be possible to then direct this flow of energy toward other beings, again in an imaginal way that offers loving-kindness outward. The purpose of the practice is to allow yourself to be a channel for a flow of loving energy to all beings, including your own self.

Sit comfortably with eyes closed and begin to notice the sensations of breath as a felt bodily experience. Then send your attention to the crown of the head. As you breathe in, imagine energy from heavenly realms entering your body through the crown of the head. Try slowing the breath down, and as the breath comes into the body, move your attention down the spinal column starting at the crown and reaching the base of the spine at the end of the in-breath. As you do this, try to actually feel sensations in the spine at the place your attention is directed. As you begin the out-breath, reverse the process and let your attention move back up the spine and up to the crown of the head as the out-breath ends. You can do exactly the same process in reverse, imaging energy coming from the earth and entering the base of the spine, moving up with the in-breath and then back down as the out-breath occurs. Both ways can be used as a concentration tool and as a tool that awakens energy and grounds attention in bodily awareness.

You can shift this practice to make it an experience related to the end of chapter 8, connecting to all beings in a loving way:

> When we recognize that what we are is Awareness (*Yud*) Connected through Loving Attention (*Vav*) to the Truth of Whatever Is Arising (*Hay*) Comprehended through Wisdom (*Hay*), we move beyond the alienation caused by the conceptualizing brain. We then see the world through the eyes of love. The unity of Exodus 33, "seeing the world through God's eyes," can also be expressed as God seeing the world through our eyes. This clear seeing and loving connection to what is seen impels us to act kindly to "Everything Unfolding in Being." This is the point of practice.

Here is the shift for you to try out. Whether starting the in-breath with attention at the crown or at the base of the spine, follow the above instructions for breathing in. On the out-breath, rather than directing the attention all the way back to the starting place, either the top or base of the spine, when you reach the place in the spine at the level of your heart, shift your attention to move from the spine to the heart center itself, and from there send your attention in any direction you wish, radiating out from the heart center. You could imagine a plane parallel to the ground at the level of your heart. Your attention as the out-breath comes to a conclusion would be moving outward in some direction along that plane and away from the heart. Eventually you can practice moving your attention in any direction away from the heart. You can even imagine all directions at once—being a fountain pouring out loving intention.

As you direct your attention and the energy it brings with it outward, you can imagine particular beings and aim the attention in their direction. With practice it is possible to experience yourself as a channel for sending Loving Attention to all beings. This is an aspect of the Divine Unfolding of Being working through what you usually think of as you. It is helpful to make this not an ego activity but rather a blessing activity in which the ego willingly takes a side seat to allow this process to unfold.

Practice 3   The Power of "And"

The practice offered here was developed by my teacher, Reb Zalman Schachter-Shalomi *z"l*. He liked to call it the *dhikr* of opposites. *Dhikr* is a form of devotional practice that Reb Zalman learned from various Sufi orders. *Dhikr* was used to cultivate devotion through the repetition of names of God and/or divine attributes. In this practice Reb Zalman used a form he had learned in the Sufi world to illuminate a particular name for God. That name is "And." We explored it in the world of *Yetzirah* or *ruach*. This is a dyad practice using spoken words. You and a partner face each other. One person starts and says a single word. Both people say the word "and" together. The second person says a word that would generally be considered an opposite of the first word. Then that second person starts the next round with a new word. Person two offers the word, both say "and," then the original first person adds the new opposite. Then switch starters again. Keep the verbal emphasis on the pairs of opposite words. Try words that easily elicit an opposite. After doing this for exercise for ninety seconds, start over. It is OK to repeat old words and/or add new ones. This time however, both people put added verbal emphasis on the word "and." See what happens when the word "and" is emphasized.

Practice 4 Sustaining Awakened Attention

Awake

> Wake up, wake up,
> Your light has come, rise and shine.
> Awaken, awaken; sing a melody,
> The glory of God will be revealed upon thee.
> FROM THE FRIDAY EVENING LITURGY, WELCOMING THE SABBATH

I'd like to share a practice that you can begin to work with as you explore the experience of being awake. It might help you steady your ability to be awake and present moment by moment. This steadying of attention is sometimes referred to as "continuity" of practice. With this steadying comes a familiarity of the experience of sustained awareness. It is also a technique that trains the mind to have some facility for working with thought as it arises in the mind by deliberately creating simple thoughts as the object of focus and then maintaining attention to the gap between thoughts. This is helpful because it is usually the all-consuming nature of the thinking process that swamps the ability to simply be aware of what is arising moment by moment. Our attention gets co-opted by the "train of thought," and we get lost on the train instead of witnessing.

This practice begins as a mantra practice. It uses the word "awakened" as the word/thought to be repeated over and over in the mind. Being fully awake is a metaphor for clearly seeing the truth of each moment of experience. It is a central theme in Jewish mystical teaching. In the Friday night liturgy we chant *Lecha Dodi* (come my beloved) as part of the *Kabbalat Shabbat* (welcoming the Sabbath) liturgy that the mystics of Safed added before the regular evening service on Friday night—the beginning of the Sabbath in Jewish practice. This prayer was composed by the mystics to explore the nature of divine unity. The fifth verse in this prayer begins with the words *Hitor'ree, hitor'ree, kee va oraych*, "Wake up, wake up! Your light has already come." The grammar of the word translated as "wake up" is the command form for oneself to be awakened. It is a reflexive verb in Hebrew. A more literal translation is "be awakened."

This is a beautiful verse in this mystic prayer because it points to a simple truth about experiencing the divine light of the world. You don't need to go somewhere to find this light. You don't need to change anything to "see the light." You simply need to wake up to what is already there. The use of the past tense in describing the coming of the light implies that it is right here and right now—not something other than "this." In creating a contemplative practice that uses the word "awakened" as its base, we are trying to use the meaning of the word to foster the process of awakening and to sustain an awakened state of mind.

Silently, in your mind, begin to chant the word "awakened." I like to do this practice by linking the repetition of the mantra to the arising and passing of the breath. As I have discussed, staying connected to the breath while doing various meditation practices keeps the experience grounded in the body and in the here and now. As you breathe in, you are preparing yourself for allowing the word to be conceptualized on the out-breath. When you breathe out, silently, in your mind, say the word "awakened."

This practice can initially be used as a process to set your intention to the wholesome desire to be awake in this life. Awake means present and witnessing the truth of the moment, paying attention to the here and now. It also implies mindful attention. Mindful attention is clear, balanced, nonjudgmental attention to the truth of the present moment of experience. In Jewish meditation as I practice it, the present moment of experience is equivalent to the Divine manifesting as the Present Moment of Being. Each time you formulate the word "awakened" in your mind, on the out-breath, you can imagine you are reminding yourself to be awake. This possibility of being awake in the moment is itself a manifestation of the Divine—awareness is an aspect of Being. And in addition, everything that is experienced from the "awake" position is also a manifestation of Being. As some steadiness of awakened presence arises, it is possible to use the space of the in-breath to simply be present to whatever is arising without adding thought in the mind. Then, with the next out-breath, the word "awakened" is repeated. For me, it becomes an affirmation that I was awake to what was noticed during the in-breath as well as a reminder to stay awake for the next moment of in-breath.

I find that this practice often tends to help me stay present for more consecutive moments. But as with any practice, my attention will wander. I tend to notice this somewhat more easily because the mantra of "awakened" disappears. If I feel a need to arouse my attention and return from being "lost on the train of thought" to the moment at hand, I will switch the mantra and begin to say, "Wake up!" Then when I feel I am back, I return to "awakened."

As I mentioned at the beginning of describing this practice, you can also use it to gain some facility with staying awake and attentive while thought is occurring. This is an important skill to cultivate, but most people find it quite difficult to do. If you work with the instruction to notice your thoughts as the object of focus in meditation, most people find that they are lost in thought rather than "witnessing" thought. That is because so many thoughts come unbidden, at a fast pace, into our minds. In this practice, we are instead deliberately thinking of just one word, one concept—"awakened." As you practice saying "awakened," try and pay attention over time in your own mind to three distinct phases. Most people can begin to recognize that there is a space in their consciousness that is knowable before the word "awakened" gets formulated and expressed in the mind. There is also the experience of consciousness of the word/concept "awakened" being expressed. This is sometimes experienced syllable by syllable or as the gestalt of the concept. Then there is the experiencing of consciousness no longer conceptualizing the word "awakened."

Working in this way it is possible to begin to know how the thinking process proceeds and what the thinking process feels like. Thinking one word at a time helps break down the thinking process to a manageable meditation experience. It is easier to keep the witnessing function going when there is only one simple word entering and leaving the mind and when you know ahead of time what that word will be and roughly when it will arise. It is analogous to using the breath as a simple object of focus in the development over time of the ability to be present in open awareness to whatever is arising. Initially, it may seem that it is one or the other, that either one is thinking or witnessing, but this practice will allow you to witness thinking. You can also experiment with witnessing increasingly longer thoughts. For example, you might switch to the thought "I am awake" on each out-breath. If you are attentive and going slowly while repeating these words in mantra fashion, you can begin to notice the different "feeling" of the thought "I am awake" from the thought "wake up" or "awakened." You can get a feel for what happens to the heart and mind as the word/thought "I" gets appended to "awake." It is possible to get a sense of witnessing the "conceptual I" arise and pass.

Sustaining careful attention to the period of the in-breath, it is also possible to begin to recognize what the mind, free of concepts, feels like. Usually, the thinking mind keeps words and concepts flowing. But in this practice, there is a deliberate stopping of the thinking mind for a short period. The period of one in-breath is a short enough time that it is often possible to briefly stop thinking, but repetitive enough to begin to get an experiential sense of what the mind, free of thought, feels like.

The purpose of this practice is to develop the ability to stay awake—that is, to be aware and present to what is unfolding in the present moment for extended periods. This is an antidote to the basic problem of being lost in the virtual reality of conceptual thinking. This practice works with both awareness itself and with an exploration of conceptual thinking. The result of awakening is also expressed in the same verse of the chant *Lecha Dodi*. The verse that begins with *Hitor'ree* ends with the line *K'vod YHVH alayich niglah*, "The glory of the Divine is revealed to you." The process of awakening allows us to experience the Divine flowing through our very Being.

Practice 5 · Where Are You in Your Life? What Is Your Heart Telling You?

This exercise is also done in dyads using spoken words. The technique used involves the repeated asking of a question. The same person asks the same question repeatedly. The second person gives an answer each time. That person can repeat a previous answer but is also encouraged to give new answers when possible. After each answer the person who asked says, "Thank you," and then repeats the question. Answers need not be given instantly, but as soon as an answer begins to arise, it should be spoken. Try not to censor your answers. Take five minutes with the same person asking. After five minutes, both people sit quietly for sixty seconds. Both people can try and be open to how they feel in the silence after this experience. Switch who begins asking. Take five more minutes with the second person asking the question. Each answer is met with a "thank you," and then the question is repeated.

For this exercise, the questions are based on the story of the expulsion from the Garden of Eden. The first question is "Where are you in your life?" Take twelve minutes for this first round: five minutes for repeated questions and different answers, and one minute of silence, repeat with the first answerer becoming the questioner for five minutes and then another minute of silence. The process then starts over with a new question. The second question is "What is your heart telling you?" Answer this question as much in the moment as possible.

Notes

Chapter 1: The Torah and the Arising of Human Consciousness

1. *Torah* is the Hebrew word for the primary sacred text of Judaism. It sometimes refers specifically to the first five books of the Hebrew Bible, and other times it is used more generally for Jewish sacred teachings or Jewish teaching all together.

Chapter 2: Speech in Exile

1. Daniel Matt, *Zohar: The Book of Enlightenment* (Ramsey, NJ: Paulist Press, 1983), 54.

2. This same notion became prevalent in early Christianity: "In the beginning was the Word, and the Word was with God, and the Word was God" (John 1:1); "I am alpha and omega [first and last letters of the Greek alphabet]" (Revelation 1:8).

3. Matt, *Zohar*, 215, notes to page 54.

4. Matt, *Zohar*, 42.

5. *Zohar* 1:24b, trans. Moshe Miller (Morristown, NJ: Fiftieth Gate Publications, 2000).

Chapter 3: What Is YHVH?

1. Menahem Nahum of Chernobyl, cited by Arthur Waskow, *Or Chadash, New Paths for Shabbat Morning* (Philadelphia: P'nai Or Religious Fellowship, 1987).

Chapter 4: The Four Worlds Model

1. My translation of Isaiah 43:7.

Chapter 5: The Human Journey

1. *Genesis Rabbah* 38:13.

Chapter 6: Toward a Culture of Holiness

1. My translation of Genesis 32:25–31.

2. Arthur Waskow, *Godwrestling—Round 2: Ancient Wisdom, Future Paths* (Woodstock, VT: Jewish Lights, 1996), 25.

3. Rev. Dr. A. Cohen, *The Soncino Chumash* (London: Soncino Press, 1983), 329–32.

Chapter 7: Saying "You" to God

1. Martin Buber, *I and Thou*, trans. Ronald Gregor Smith (New York: Charles Scribner's Sons, 1958), 3.

2. Ibid.

3. Ibid., 4.

4. Ibid., 76.

5. Ibid., 6.

6. "Where Can I Not Find You: Opening the Emotional Channel to Divine," by Jeff Roth, *Awakened Heart Project*, podcast audio, 10:28, December 30, 2011, http://www.awakenedheartproject.org/podcasts/where-can-i-not-find-you-opening-the-emotional-channel-to-divine.

Chapter 8: Living with an Awakened Heart

1. For a more expanded explanation of this event, see my previous book: Jeff Roth, *Jewish Meditation Practices for Everyday Life* (Woodstock, VT: Jewish Lights, 2009), 130–33.

2. David Wolfe-Blank, *The Aquarian Minyan Mahzor* (Berkeley, CA: Aquarian Minyan, 1981), translation of Exodus 34:6–7.

3. My translation of Genesis 3:6–9.

4. For a full explanation of this practice, see my book *Jewish Meditation Practices for Everyday Life*, 163–82.

Suggestions for
Further Reading

Boorstein, Sylvia. *That's Funny, You Don't Look Buddhist*. San Francisco: HarperSanFrancisco, 1997.

Buber, Martin. *I and Thou*. Translated by Ronald Gregor Smith. New York: Charles Scribner's Sons, 1958.

Cooper, David. *God Is a Verb: Kabbalah and the Practice of Mystical Judaism*. New York: Riverhead Books, 1997.

Fischer, Norman. *Opening to You: Zen-Inspired Translations of the Psalms*. New York: Penguin, 2002.

Green, Arthur. Ehyeh: *A Kabbalah for Tomorrow*. Woodstock, VT: Jewish Lights, 2003.

———. *Radical Judaism: Rethinking God and Transformation*. New Haven, CT: Yale University Press, 2010.

Jaynes, Julian. *The Origin of Consciousness in the Breakdown of the Bicameral Mind*. Boston: Houghton Mifflin, 1976.

Lew, Alan. *This Is Real and You Are Completely Unprepared: The Days of Awe as a Journey of Transformation*. Boston: Little, Brown, 2003.

Michaelson, Jay. *Everything Is God: The Radical Path of Nondual Judaism*. Boston: Trumpeter, 2009.

Roth, Jeff. *Jewish Meditation Practices for Everyday Life: Awakening Your Heart, Connecting with God*. Woodstock, VT: Jewish Lights, 2009.

Schachter-Shalomi, Zalman. *Gates to the Heart: A Manual of Contemplative Jewish Practice*. Boulder, CO: Albion-Andalus Books, 2013.

Bible Study / Midrash

Passing Life's Tests: Spiritual Reflections on the Trial of Abraham, the Binding of Isaac *By Rabbi Bradley Shavit Artson, DHL*
Invites us to use this powerful tale as a tool for our own soul wrestling, to confront our existential sacrifices and enable us to face—and surmount—life's tests.
6 x 9, 176 pp, Quality PB, 978-1-58023-631-7 **$18.99**

Speaking Torah: Spiritual Teachings from around the Maggid's Table—in Two Volumes *By Arthur Green, with Ebn Leader, Ariel Evan Mayse and Or N. Rose*
The most powerful Hasidic teachings made accessible—from some of the world's preeminent authorities on Jewish thought and spirituality.
Volume 1—6 x 9, 512 pp, HC, 978-1-58023-668-3 **$34.99**
Volume 2—6 x 9, 448 pp, HC, 978-1-58023-694-2 **$34.99**

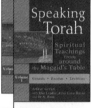

A Partner in Holiness: Deepening Mindfulness, Practicing Compassion and Enriching Our Lives through the Wisdom of R. Levi Yitzhak of Berdichev's *Kedushat Levi*
By Rabbi Jonathan P. Slater, DMin; Foreword by Arthur Green; Preface by Rabby Nancy Flam
Contemporary mindfulness and classical Hasidic spirituality are brought together to inspire a satisfying spiritual life of practice.
Volume 1—6 x 9, 336 pp, HC, 978-1-58023-794-9 **$35.00**
Volume 2—6 x 9, 288 pp, HC, 978-1-58023-795-6 **$35.00**

The Genesis of Leadership: What the Bible Teaches Us about Vision, Values and Leading Change *By Rabbi Nathan Laufer; Foreword by Senator Joseph I. Lieberman*
6 x 9, 288 pp, Quality PB, 978-1-58023-352-1 **$18.99**

Hineini in Our Lives: Learning How to Respond to Others through 14 Biblical Texts and Personal Stories *By Dr. Norman J. Cohen* 6 x 9, 240 pp, Quality PB, 978-1-58023-274-6 **$18.99**

Masking and Unmasking Ourselves: Interpreting Biblical Texts on Clothing & Identity *By Dr. Norman J. Cohen* 6 x 9, 224 pp, HC, 978-1-58023-461-0 **$24.99**
Quality PB, 978-1-58023-839-7 **$18.99**

The Messiah and the Jews: Three Thousand Years of Tradition, Belief and Hope
By Rabbi Elaine Rose Glickman; Foreword by Rabbi Neil Gillman, PhD
Preface by Rabbi Judith Z. Abrams, PhD 6 x 9, 192 pp, Quality PB, 978-1-58023-690-4 **$16.99**

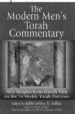

The Modern Men's Torah Commentary: New Insights from Jewish Men on the 54 Weekly Torah Portions *Edited by Rabbi Jeffrey K. Salkin*
6 x 9, 368 pp, HC, 978-1-58023-395-8 **$24.99**

Moses and the Journey to Leadership: Timeless Lessons of Effective Management from the Bible and Today's Leaders *By Dr. Norman J. Cohen*
6 x 9, 240 pp, Quality PB, 978-1-58023-351-4 **$18.99**; HC, 978-1-58023-227-2 **$21.99**

The Other Talmud—The *Yerushalmi*: Unlocking the Secrets of *The Talmud of Israel* for Judaism Today *By Rabbi Judith Z. Abrams, PhD*
6 x 9, 256 pp, HC, 978-1-58023-463-4 **$24.99**

Sage Tales: Wisdom and Wonder from the Rabbis of the Talmud
By Rabbi Burton L. Visotzky
6 x 9, 256 pp, Quality PB, 978-1-58023-791-8 **$19.99**; HC, 978-1-58023-456-6 **$24.99**

The Torah Revolution: Fourteen Truths That Changed the World
By Rabbi Reuven Hammer, PhD 6 x 9, 240 pp, Quality PB, 978-1-58023-789-5 **$18.99**
HC, 978-1-58023-457-3 **$24.99**

The Wisdom of Judaism: An Introduction to the Values of the Talmud
By Rabbi Dov Peretz Elkins 6 x 9, 192 pp, Quality PB, 978-1-58023-327-9 **$16.99**

Or phone, fax, mail or email to: **JEWISH LIGHTS** Publishing
Sunset Farm Offices, Route 4 • P.O. Box 237 • Woodstock, Vermont 05091
Tel: (802) 457-4000 • Fax: (802) 457-4004 • www.jewishlights.com
Credit card orders: **(800) 962-4544** (8:30AM–5:30PM EST Monday–Friday)
Generous discounts on quantity orders. SATISFACTION GUARANTEED. Prices subject to change.

Spirituality / Prayer

Davening: A Guide to Meaningful Jewish Prayer
By Rabbi Zalman Schachter-Shalomi (z"l) with Joel Segel; Foreword by Rabbi Lawrence Kushner
A fresh approach to prayer for all who wish to appreciate the power of prayer's
poetry, song and ritual, and to join the age-old conversation that Jews have had
with God. 6 x 9, 240 pp, Quality PB, 978-1-58023-627-0 **$18.99**

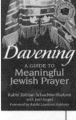

Jewish Men Pray: Words of Yearning, Praise, Petition, Gratitude and
Wonder from Traditional and Contemporary Sources
Edited by Rabbi Kerry M. Olitzky and Stuart M. Matlins; Foreword by Rabbi Bradley Shavit Artson, DHL
A celebration of Jewish men's voices in prayer—to strengthen, heal, comfort, and
inspire—from the ancient world up to our own day.
5 x 7¼, 400 pp, HC, 978-1-58023-628-7 **$19.99**

Making Prayer Real: Leading Jewish Spiritual Voices on Why Prayer Is Difficult and What
to Do about It *By Rabbi Mike Comins* 6 x 9, 320 pp, Quality PB, 978-1-58023-417-7 **$18.99**

Witnesses to the One: The Spiritual History of the *Sh'ma*
By Rabbi Joseph B. Meszler; Foreword by Rabbi Elyse Goldstein
6 x 9, 176 pp, Quality PB, 978-1-58023-400-9 **$16.99**; HC, 978-1-58023-309-5 **$19.99**

My People's Prayer Book Series: Traditional Prayers, Modern
Commentaries *Edited by Rabbi Lawrence A. Hoffman, PhD*
Provides diverse and exciting commentary to the traditional liturgy. Will help you
find new wisdom in Jewish prayer, and bring liturgy into your life. Each book
includes Hebrew text, modern translations and commentaries from all perspectives
of the Jewish world.
- Vol. 1—The *Sh'ma* and Its Blessings
  7 x 10, 168 pp, HC, 978-1-879045-79-8 **$29.99**
- Vol. 2—The *Amidah* 7 x 10, 240 pp, HC, 978-1-879045-80-4 **$29.99**
- Vol. 3—*P'sukei D'zimrah* (Morning Psalms)
  7 x 10, 240 pp, HC, 978-1-879045-81-1 **$35.00**
- Vol. 4—*Seder K'riat Hatorah* (The Torah Service)
  7 x 10, 264 pp, HC, 978-1-879045-82-8 **$29.99**
- Vol. 5—*Birkhot Hashachar* (Morning Blessings)
  7 x 10, 240 pp, HC, 978-1-879045-83-5 **$35.00**
- Vol. 6—*Tachanun* and Concluding Prayers
  7 x 10, 240 pp, HC, 978-1-879045-84-2 **$24.95**
- Vol. 7—Shabbat at Home 7 x 10, 240 pp, HC, 978-1-879045-85-9 **$29.99**
- Vol. 8—*Kabbalat Shabbat* (Welcoming Shabbat in the Synagogue)
  7 x 10, 240 pp, HC, 978-1-58023-121-3 **$24.99**
- Vol. 9—Welcoming the Night: *Minchah* and *Ma'ariv* (Afternoon and
  Evening Prayer) 7 x 10, 272 pp, HC, 978-1-58023-262-3 **$35.00**
- Vol. 10—Shabbat Morning: *Shacharit* and *Musaf* (Morning and
  Additional Services) 7 x 10, 240 pp, HC, 978-1-58023-240-1 **$35.00**

Spirituality / Lawrence Kushner

I'm God; You're Not: Observations on Organized Religion & Other Disguises of the Ego
6 x 9, 256 pp, Quality PB, 978-1-58023-513-6 **$18.99**; HC, 978-1-58023-441-2 **$21.99**

The Book of Letters: A Mystical Hebrew Alphabet
Popular HC Edition 6 x 9, 80 pp, 2-color text, 978-1-879045-00-2 **$24.95**
Collector's Limited Edition 9 x 12, 80 pp, gold-foil-embossed pages, w/ limited-edition silk-
screened print, 978-1-879045-04-0 **$349.00**

The Book of Miracles: A Young Person's Guide to Jewish Spiritual Awareness
6 x 9, 96 pp, 2-color illus., HC, 978-1-879045-78-1 **$16.95** *For ages 9–13*

God Was in This Place & I, i Did Not Know: Finding Self, Spirituality and
Ultimate Meaning 6 x 9, 192 pp, Quality PB, 978-1-879045-33-0 **$18.99**

Honey from the Rock: An Introduction to Jewish Mysticism
6 x 9, 176 pp, Quality PB, 978-1-58023-073-5 **$18.99**

Invisible Lines of Connection: Sacred Stories of the Ordinary
5½ x 8½, 160 pp, Quality PB, 978-1-879045-98-9 **$16.99**

The Way Into Jewish Mystical Tradition
6 x 9, 224 pp, Quality PB, 978-1-58023-200-5 **$18.99**

Theology / Philosophy

Renewing the Process of Creation: A Jewish Integration of Science and Spirit *By Rabbi Bradley Shavit Artson, DHL*
A daring blend of Jewish theology, science and Process Thought, exploring personal actions through Judaism and the sciences as dynamically interactive and mutually informative. 6 x 9, 208 pp, HC, 978-1-58023-833-5 **$24.99**

Does the Soul Survive? 2nd Edition: A Jewish Journey to Belief in Afterlife, Past Lives & Living with Purpose *By Rabbi Elie Kaplan Spitz*
Foreword by Brian L. Weiss, MD A skeptic turned believer recounts his quest to uncover the Jewish tradition's answers about what happens to our souls after death.
6 x 9, 288 pp, Quality PB, 978-1-58023-818-2 **$18.99**

God of Becoming and Relationship: The Dynamic Nature of Process Theology *By Rabbi Bradley Shavit Artson, DHL* Explains how Process Theology breaks us free from the strictures of ancient Greek and medieval European philosophy. 6 x 9, 208 pp, HC, 978-1-58023-713-0 **$24.99**

The Way of Man: According to Hasidic Teaching
By Martin Buber; New Translation and Introduction by Rabbi Bernard H. Mehlman and Dr. Gabriel E. Padawer; Foreword by Paul Mendes-Flohr
An accessible and engaging new translation of Buber's classic work—*available as an eBook only.* eBook, 978-1-58023-601-0 **$18.99**

Believing and Its Tensions: A Personal Conversation about God, Torah, Suffering and Death in Jewish Thought *By Rabbi Neil Gillman, PhD*
5½ x 8½, 144 pp, HC, 978-1-58023-669-0 **$19.99**

The Death of Death: Resurrection and Immortality in Jewish Thought
By Rabbi Neil Gillman, PhD   6 x 9, 336 pp, Quality PB, 978-1-58023-081-0 **$19.99**

From Defender to Critic: The Search for a New Jewish Self
By Dr. David Hartman (z"l)   6 x 9, 336 pp, HC, 978-1-58023-515-0 **$35.00**

The God Who Hates Lies: Confronting & Rethinking Jewish Tradition
By Dr. David Hartman (z"l) with Charlie Buckholtz   6 x 9, 208 pp, Quality PB, 978-1-58023-790-1 **$19.99**

A Heart of Many Rooms: Celebrating the Many Voices within Judaism
By Dr. David Hartman (z"l)   6 x 9, 352 pp, Quality PB, 978-1-58023-156-5 **$24.99**

Jewish Theology in Our Time: A New Generation Explores the Foundations and Future of Jewish Belief *Edited by Rabbi Elliot J. Cosgrove, PhD; Foreword by Rabbi David J. Wolpe*
Preface by Rabbi Carole B. Balin, PhD
6 x 9, 240 pp, Quality PB, 978-1-58023-630-0 **$19.99**; HC, 978-1-58023-413-9 **$24.99**

Maimonides—Essential Teachings on Jewish Faith & Ethics: The Book of Knowledge & the Thirteen Principles of Faith—Annotated & Explained
Translation and Annotation by Rabbi Marc D. Angel, PhD
5½ x 8½, 224 pp, Quality PB, 978-1-59473-311-6 **$18.99***

Our Religious Brains: What Cognitive Science Reveals about Belief, Mortality, Community and Our Relationship with God *By Rabbi Ralph D. Mecklenburger;*
Foreword by Dr. Howard Kelfer; Preface by Dr. Neil Gillman
6 x 9, 224 pp, HC, 978-1-58023-508-2 **$24.99**; Quality PB, 978-1-58023-840-3 **$18.99**

God, Faith & Identity from the Ashes
Reflections of Children and Grandchildren of Holocaust Survivors
Almost ninety contributors from sixteen countries inform, challenge and inspire people of all backgrounds. *Edited by Menachem Z. Rosensaft; Prologue by Elie Wiesel*
6 x 9, 352 pp, HC, 978-1-58023-805-2 **$25.00**

I Am Jewish
Personal Reflections Inspired by the Last Words of Daniel Pearl
Almost 150 Jews—both famous and not—from all walks of life, from all around the world, write about many aspects of their Judaism.
Edited by Judea and Ruth Pearl   6 x 9, 304 pp, Deluxe PB w/ flaps, 978-1-58023-259-3 **$19.99**
Download a free copy of the *I Am Jewish Teacher's Guide* at www.jewishlights.com.

**A book from SkyLight Paths, Jewish Lights' sister imprint*

Inspiration

The Best Boy in the United States of America
A Memoir of Blessings and Kisses *By Dr. Ron Wolfson*
Will resonate with anyone seeking to shape stronger families and communities and live a life of joy and purpose.   6 x 9, 192 pp, HC, 978-1-58023-838-0 **$19.99**

The Chutzpah Imperative: Empowering Today's Jews for a Life
That Matters *By Rabbi Edward Feinstein; Foreword by Rabbi Laura Geller*
A new view of chutzpah as Jewish self-empowerment to be God's partner and repair the world. Reveals Judaism's ancient message, its deepest purpose and most precious treasures.   6 x 9, 192 pp, HC, 978-1-58023-792-5 **$21.99**

Judaism's Ten Best Ideas: A Brief Guide for Seekers
By Rabbi Arthur Green, PhD A highly accessible introduction to Judaism's greatest contributions to civilization, drawing on Jewish mystical tradition and the author's experience.   4½ x 6½, 112 pp, Quality PB, 978-1-58023-803-8 **$9.99**

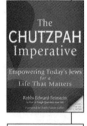

The Empty Chair: Finding Hope and Joy—Timeless Wisdom from a Hasidic Master,
Rebbe Nachman of Breslov *Adapted by Moshe Mykoff and the Breslov Research Institute*
4 x 6, 128 pp, Deluxe PB w/ flaps, 978-1-879045-67-5 **$9.99**

The Gentle Weapon: Prayers for Everyday and Not-So-Everyday Moments—
Timeless Wisdom from the Teachings of the Hasidic Master Rebbe Nachman of Breslov
Adapted by Moshe Mykoff and S. C. Mizrahi, together with the Breslov Research Institute
4 x 6, 144 pp, Deluxe PB w/ flaps, 978-1-58023-022-3 **$9.99**

God Whispers: Stories of the Soul, Lessons of the Heart   *By Rabbi Karyn D. Kedar*
6 x 9, 176 pp, Quality PB, 978-1-58023-088-9 **$16.99**

God's To-Do List: 103 Ways to Be an Angel and Do God's Work on Earth
By Dr. Ron Wolfson 6 x 9, 144 pp, Quality PB, 978-1-58023-301-9 **$16.99**

Happiness and the Human Spirit: The Spirituality of Becoming the Best You Can Be
By Rabbi Abraham J. Twerski, MD
6 x 9, 176 pp, Quality PB, 978-1-58023-404-7 **$16.99**; HC, 978-1-58023-343-9 **$19.99**

Life's Daily Blessings: Inspiring Reflections on Gratitude and Joy for Every Day,
Based on Jewish Wisdom *By Rabbi Kerry M. Olitzky*
4½ x 6½, 368 pp, Quality PB, 978-1-58023-396-5 **$16.99**

Sacred Intentions: Morning Inspiration to Strengthen the Spirit, Based on Jewish Wisdom
By Rabbi Kerry M. Olitzky and Rabbi Lori Forman-Jacobi
4½ x 6½, 448 pp, Quality PB, 978-1-58023-061-2 **$16.99**

The Seven Questions You're Asked in Heaven: Reviewing and Renewing Your
Life on Earth *By Dr. Ron Wolfson* 6 x 9, 176 pp, Quality PB, 978-1-58023-407-8 **$16.99**

Kabbalah / Mysticism

Walking the Path of the Jewish Mystic: How to Expand Your
Awareness and Transform Your Life *By Rabbi Yoel Glick*
A unique guide to the nature of both physical and spiritual reality.
6 x 9, 224 pp, Quality PB, 978-1-58023-843-4 **$18.99**

Ehyeh: A Kabbalah for Tomorrow
By Rabbi Arthur Green, PhD 6 x 9, 224 pp, Quality PB, 978-1-58023-213-5 **$18.99**

The Gift of Kabbalah: Discovering the Secrets of Heaven, Renewing Your Life on Earth
By Tamar Frankiel, PhD 6 x 9, 256 pp, Quality PB, 978-1-58023-141-1 **$18.99**

Jewish Mysticism and the Spiritual Life: Classical Texts, Contemporary
Reflections *Edited by Dr. Lawrence Fine, Dr. Eitan Fishbane and Rabbi Or N. Rose*
6 x 9, 256 pp, Quality PB, 978-1-58023-719-2 **$18.99**

Seek My Face: A Jewish Mystical Theology   *By Rabbi Arthur Green, PhD*
6 x 9, 304 pp, Quality PB, 978-1-58023-130-5 **$19.95**

Zohar: Annotated & Explained   *Translation & Annotation by Dr. Daniel C. Matt*
Foreword by Andrew Harvey 5½ x 8½, 176 pp, Quality PB, 978-1-893361-51-5 **$18.99**
(A book from SkyLight Paths, Jewish Lights' sister imprint)

See also *The Way Into Jewish Mystical Tradition* in The Way Into... Series

Children's Books by Sandy Eisenberg Sasso

The *Shema* in the Mezuzah
Listening to Each Other
Introduces children ages 3 to 6 to the words of the *Shema* and the custom of putting up the mezuzah. Winner, National Jewish Book Award.
9 x 12, 32 pp, Full-color illus., HC, 978-1-58023-506-8 **$18.99** *For ages 3–6*

Adam & Eve's First Sunset
God's New Day
Explores fear and hope, faith and gratitude in ways that will delight kids and adults—inspiring us to bless each of God's days and nights.
9 x 12, 32 pp, Full-color illus., HC, 978-1-58023-177-0 **$17.95** *For ages 4 & up*

Also Available as a Board Book: **Adam and Eve's New Day**
5 x 5, 24 pp, Full-color illus., Board Book, 978-1-59473-205-8 **$7.99*** *For ages 1–4*

But God Remembered
Stories of Women from Creation to the Promised Land
Four different stories of women—Lilith, Serach, Bityah and the Daughters of Z— teach us important values through their faith and actions.
9 x 12, 32 pp, Full-color illus., Quality PB, 978-1-58023-372-9 **$8.99** *For ages 8 & up*

For Heaven's Sake
Heaven is often found where you least expect it.
9 x 12, 32 pp, Full-color illus., HC, 978-1-58023-054-4 **$16.95** *For ages 4 & up*

God Said Amen
An inspiring story about hearing the answers to our prayers.
9 x 12, 32 pp, Full-color illus., HC, 978-1-58023-080-3 **$16.95** *For ages 4 & up*

God's Paintbrush: Special 10th Anniversary Edition
Wonderfully interactive, invites children of all faiths and backgrounds to encounter God through moments in their own lives. Provides questions adult and child can explore together.   11 x 8½, 32 pp, Full-color illus., HC, 978-1-58023-195-4 **$18.99** *For ages 4 & up*

Also Available as a Board Book: **I Am God's Paintbrush**
5 x 5, 24 pp, Full-color illus., Board Book, 978-1-59473-265-2 **$7.99*** *For ages 1–4*

Also Available: **God's Paintbrush Teacher's Guide**
8½ x 11, 32 pp, PB, 978-1-879045-57-6 **$8.95**

God's Paintbrush Celebration Kit
A Spiritual Activity Kit for Teachers and Students of All Faiths, All Backgrounds
9½ x 12, 40 Full-color Activity Sheets & Teacher Folder w/ complete instructions
HC, 978-1-58023-050-6 **$21.95**
8-Student Activity Sheet Pack (40 sheets/5 sessions), 978-1-58023-058-2 **$19.95**
Single-Student Activity Sheet Pack (5 sessions), 978-1-58023-059-9 **$3.95**

In God's Name
Like an ancient myth in its poetic text and vibrant illustrations, this award-winning modern fable about the search for God's name celebrates the diversity and, at the same time, the unity of all people.
9 x 12, 32 pp, Full-color illus., HC, 978-1-879045-26-2 **$18.99** *For ages 4 & up*

Also Available as a Board Book: **What Is God's Name?**
5 x 5, 24 pp, Full-color illus., Board Book, 978-1-893361-10-2 **$8.99*** *For ages 1–4*
Also Available in Spanish: **El nombre de Dios**
9 x 12, 32 pp, Full-color illus., HC, 978-1-893361-63-8 **$16.95** *For ages 4 & up*

Noah's Wife
The Story of Naamah
When God tells Noah to bring the animals of the world onto the ark, God also calls on Naamah, Noah's wife, to save each plant on earth.
9 x 12, 32 pp, Full-color illus., HC, 978-1-58023-134-3 **$16.95** *For ages 4 & up*

Also Available as a Board Book: **Naamah, Noah's Wife**
5 x 5, 24 pp, Full-color illus., Board Book, 978-1-893361-56-0 **$7.95*** *For ages 1–4*

**A book from SkyLight Paths, Jewish Lights' sister imprint*

Social Justice

Where Justice Dwells
A Hands-On Guide to Doing Social Justice in Your Jewish Community
By Rabbi Jill Jacobs; Foreword by Rabbi David Saperstein
Provides ways to envision and act on your own ideals of social justice.
7 x 9, 288 pp, Quality PB, 978-1-58023-453-5 **$24.99**

There Shall Be No Needy
Pursuing Social Justice through Jewish Law and Tradition
By Rabbi Jill Jacobs; Foreword by Rabbi Elliot N. Dorff, PhD; Preface by Simon Greer
Confronts the most pressing issues of twenty-first-century America from a deeply Jewish perspective. 6 x 9, 288 pp, Quality PB, 978-1-58023-425-2 **$16.99**

There Shall Be No Needy Teacher's Guide 8½ x 11, 56 pp, PB, 978-1-58023-429-0 **$8.99**

Conscience
The Duty to Obey and the Duty to Disobey
By Rabbi Harold M. Schulweis (z"l)
Examines the idea of conscience and the role conscience plays in our relationships to government, law, ethics, religion, human nature, God—and to each other.
6 x 9, 160 pp, Quality PB, 978-1-58023-419-1 **$16.99**; HC, 978-1-58023-375-0 **$19.99**

Judaism and Justice: The Jewish Passion to Repair the World
By Rabbi Sidney Schwarz; Foreword by Ruth Messinger
6 x 9, 352 pp, Quality PB, 978-1-58023-353-8 **$19.99**

Spirituality / Women's Interest

Embracing the Divine Feminine: Finding God through the Ecstasy of Physical Love—The Song of Songs Annotated & Explained
Annotation and Translation by Rabbi Rami Shapiro; Foreword by Rev. Cynthia Bourgeault, PhD
Restores the Song of Songs' eroticism and interprets it as a celebration of the love between the Divine Feminine and the contemporary spiritual seeker.
5½ x 8½, 176 pp, Quality PB, 978-1-59473-575-2 **$16.99***

The Women's Haftarah Commentary
New Insights from Women Rabbis on the 54 Weekly Haftarah Portions, the 5 Megillot & Special Shabbatot
Edited by Rabbi Elyse Goldstein
Illuminates the historical significance of female portrayals in the Haftarah and the Five Megillot. 6 x 9, 560 pp, Quality PB, 978-1-58023-371-2 **$19.99**

The Women's Torah Commentary
New Insights from Women Rabbis on the 54 Weekly Torah Portions
Edited by Rabbi Elyse Goldstein
Over fifty women rabbis offer inspiring insights on the Torah, in a week-by-week format.
6 x 9, 496 pp, Quality PB, 978-1-58023-370-5 **$19.99**

The Divine Feminine in Biblical Wisdom Literature
Selections Annotated & Explained
Translation & Annotation by Rabbi Rami Shapiro; Foreword by Rev. Cynthia Bourgeault, PhD
5½ x 8½, 240 pp, Quality PB, 978-1-59473-109-9 **$18.99***

New Jewish Feminism: Probing the Past, Forging the Future
Edited by Rabbi Elyse Goldstein; Foreword by Anita Diamant
6 x 9, 480 pp, HC, 978-1-58023-359-0 **$24.99**

The Quotable Jewish Woman
Wisdom, Inspiration & Humor from the Mind & Heart
Edited by Elaine Bernstein Partnow
6 x 9, 496 pp, Quality PB, 978-1-58023-236-4 **$19.99**

See *Passover* for *The Women's Passover Companion: Women's Reflections on the Festival of Freedom* and *The Women's Seder Sourcebook: Rituals & Readings for Use at the Passover Seder.*

**A book from SkyLight Paths, Jewish Lights' sister imprint*

Congregation Resources

Disaster Spiritual Care, 2nd Edition
Practical Clergy Responses to Community, Regional and National Tragedy
Edited by Rabbi Stephen B. Roberts, BCJC, and Rev. Willard W. C. Ashley Sr., DMin, DH
Updated and expanded—the definitive guidebook for counseling not only the victims of disaster but also the clergy and caregivers who are called to service in the wake of a crisis. 6 x 9, 384 pp (est), HC, 978-1-59473-587-5 **$50.00***

Jewish Ethical Values: A Sourcebook of Classic Texts and Their
Practical Uses for Our Lives *By Dr. Byron L. Sherwin and Dr. Seymour J. Cohen*
Offers selections from classic Jewish ethical literature and clear explanations of their historic context of each writing and thoughtful applications of their wisdom for our lives today. 6 x 9, 336 pp, Quality PB, 978-1-58023-835-9 **$19.99**

New Membership & Financial Alternatives for the American
Synagogue From Traditional Dues to Fair Share to Gifts from the Heart
By Rabbi Kerry M. Olitzky and Rabbi Avi S. Olitzky; Foreword by Dr. Ron Wolfson
Afterword by Rabbi Dan Judson Practice values-driven ways to make changes to open wide the synagogue doors to many. 6 x 9, 208 pp, Quality PB, 978-1-58023-820-5 **$19.99**

Relational Judaism: Using the Power of Relationships to Transform
the Jewish Community *By Dr. Ron Wolfson* How to transform the model of twentieth-century Jewish institutions into twenty-first-century relational communities offering meaning and purpose, belonging and blessing.
6 x 9, 288 pp, HC, 978-1-58023-666-9 **$24.99**

The Spirituality of Welcoming: How to Transform Your
Congregation into a Sacred Community *By Dr. Ron Wolfson*
Shows crucial hospitality is for congregational survival and dives into the practicalities of cultivating openness.
6 x 9, 224 pp, Quality PB, 978-1-58023-244-9 **$19.99**

Jewish Megatrends: Charting the Course of the American Jewish Future
By Rabbi Sidney Schwarz; Foreword by Ambassador Stuart E. Eizenstat
Visionary solutions for a community ripe for transformational change—from fourteen leading innovators of Jewish life. 6 x 9, 288 pp, HC, 978-1-58023-667-6 **$24.99**

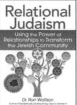

Building a Successful Volunteer Culture: Finding Meaning in Service in the Jewish Community *By Rabbi Charles Simon; Foreword by Shelley Lindauer; Preface by Dr. Ron Wolfson*
6 x 9, 192 pp, Quality PB, 978-1-58023-408-5 **$16.99**

Empowered Judaism: What Independent Minyanim Can Teach Us about Building Vibrant Jewish Communities *By Rabbi Elie Kaunfer; Foreword by Prof. Jonathan D. Sarna*
6 x 9, 224 pp, Quality PB, 978-1-58023-412-2 **$18.99**

Inspired Jewish Leadership: Practical Approaches to Building Strong Communities
By Dr. Erica Brown 6 x 9, 256 pp, HC, 978-1-58023-361-3 **$27.99**

Judaism and Health: A Handbook of Practical, Professional and Scholarly Resources
Edited by Jeff Levin, PhD, MPH, and Michele F. Prince, LCSW, MAJCS
Foreword by Rabbi Elliot N. Dorff, PhD 6 x 9, 448 pp, HC, 978-1-58023-714-7 **$50.00**

Jewish Pastoral Care, 2nd Edition: A Practical Handbook from Traditional & Contemporary Sources *Edited by Rabbi Dayle A. Friedman, MSW, MA, BCC*
6 x 9, 528 pp, Quality PB, 978-1-58023-427-6 **$35.00**

A Practical Guide to Rabbinic Counseling
Edited by Rabbi Yisrael N. Levitz, PhD, and Rabbi Abraham J. Twerski, MD
6 x 9, 432 pp, HC, 978-1-58023-562-4 **$40.00**

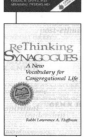

Professional Spiritual & Pastoral Care: A Practical Clergy and Chaplain's Handbook
Edited by Rabbi Stephen B. Roberts, MBA, MHL, BCJC 6 x 9, 480 pp, HC, 978-1-59473-312-3 **$50.00***

Reimagining Leadership in Jewish Organizations: Ten Practical Lessons to Help You Implement Change and Achieve Your Goals
By Dr. Misha Galperin 6 x 9, 192 pp, Quality PB, 978-1-58023-492-4 **$16.99**

Rethinking Synagogues: A New Vocabulary for Congregational Life
By Rabbi Lawrence A. Hoffman, PhD 6 x 9, 240 pp, Quality PB, 978-1-58023-248-7 **$19.99**

*A book from SkyLight Paths, Jewish Lights' sister imprint

Holidays / Holy Days

Prayers of Awe Series

An exciting new series that examines the High Holy Day liturgy to enrich the praying experience of everyone—whether experienced worshipers or guests who encounter Jewish prayer for the very first time. *Edited by Rabbi Lawrence A. Hoffman, PhD*

Who by Fire, Who by Water—*Un'taneh Tokef*
6 x 9, 272 pp, Quality PB, 978-1-58023-672-0 **$19.99**; HC, 978-1-58023-424-5 **$24.99**

All These Vows—*Kol Nidre*
6 x 9, 288 pp, HC, 978-1-58023-430-6 **$24.99**

We Have Sinned—Sin and Confession in Judaism: *Ashamnu* and *Al Chet*
6 x 9, 304 pp, HC, 978-1-58023-612-6 **$24.99**

May God Remember: Memory and Memorializing in Judaism—*Yizkor*
6 x 9, 304 pp, HC, 978-1-58023-689-8 **$24.99**

All the World: Universalism, Particularism and the High Holy Days
6 x 9, 288 pp, HC, 978-1-58023-783-3 **$24.99**

Naming God

Avinu Malkeinu—Our Father, Our King
Edited by Rabbi Lawrence A. Hoffman, PhD
Almost forty contributors from the US, Israel, UK, Europe and Canada examine one of Judaism's favorite prayers and provide analysis of the age-old but altogether modern problem of naming God. 6 x 9, 336 pp, HC, 978-1-58023-817-5 **$27.99**

Rosh Hashanah Readings: Inspiration, Information and Contemplation
Yom Kippur Readings: Inspiration, Information and Contemplation
Edited by Rabbi Dov Peretz Elkins; Section Introductions from Arthur Green's These Are the Words
Rosh Hashanah: 6 x 9, 400 pp, Quality PB, 978-1-58023-437-5 **$19.99**
Yom Kippur: 6 x 9, 368 pp, Quality PB, 978-1-58023-438-2 **$19.99**; HC, 978-1-58023-271-5 **$24.99**

Shabbat, 2nd Edition: The Family Guide to Preparing for and Celebrating the Sabbath
By Dr. Ron Wolfson 7 x 9, 320 pp, Illus., Quality PB, 978-1-58023-164-0 **$21.99**

Hanukkah, 2nd Edition: The Family Guide to Spiritual Celebration
By Dr. Ron Wolfson 7 x 9, 240 pp, Illus., Quality PB, 978-1-58023-122-0 **$18.95**

Passover

My People's Passover Haggadah

Traditional Texts, Modern Commentaries
Edited by Rabbi Lawrence A. Hoffman, PhD, and David Arnow, PhD
A diverse and exciting collection of commentaries on the traditional Passover Haggadah—in two volumes!
Vol. 1: 7 x 10, 304 pp, HC, 978-1-58023-354-5 **$24.99**
Vol. 2: 7 x 10, 320 pp, HC, 978-1-58023-346-0 **$24.99**

Creating Lively Passover Seders, 2nd Edition: A Sourcebook of Engaging Tales, Texts & Activities *By David Arnow, PhD* 7 x 9, 464 pp, Quality PB, 978-1-58023-444-3 **$24.99**

Freedom Journeys: The Tale of Exodus and Wilderness across Millennia
By Rabbi Arthur O. Waskow and Rabbi Phyllis O. Berman
6 x 9, 288 pp, HC, 978-1-58023-445-0 **$24.99**

Leading the Passover Journey: The Seder's Meaning Revealed, the Haggadah's Story Retold *By Rabbi Nathan Laufer*
6 x 9, 224 pp, Quality PB, 978-1-58023-399-6 **$18.99**

Passover, 2nd Edition: The Family Guide to Spiritual Celebration
By Dr. Ron Wolfson with Joel Lurie Grishaver 7 x 9, 416 pp, Quality PB, 978-1-58023-174-9 **$19.95**

The Women's Passover Companion: Women's Reflections on the Festival of Freedom
Edited by Rabbi Sharon Cohen Anisfeld, Tara Mohr and Catherine Spector
Foreword by Paula E. Hyman
6 x 9, 352 pp, Quality PB, 978-1-58023-231-9 **$19.99**; HC, 978-1-58023-128-2 **$24.95**

The Women's Seder Sourcebook: Rituals & Readings for Use at the Passover Seder
Edited by Rabbi Sharon Cohen Anisfeld, Tara Mohr and Catherine Spector
6 x 9, 384 pp, Quality PB, 978-1-58023-232-6 **$19.99**

Spirituality

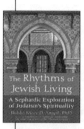

The Rhythms of Jewish Living
A Sephardic Exploration of Judaism's Spirituality
By Rabbi Marc D. Angel, PhD Reclaims the natural, balanced and insightful teachings of Sephardic Judaism that can and should imbue modern Jewish spirituality.
6 x 9, 208 pp, Quality PB, 978-1-58023-834-2 **$18.99**

God and the Big Bang, 2nd Edition
Discovering Harmony between Science and Spirituality
By Daniel C. Matt Updated and expanded. Draws on the insights of physics and Kabbalah to uncover the sense of wonder and oneness that connects humankind with the universe and God. 6 x 9, 224 pp, Quality PB, 978-1-58023-836-6 **$18.99**

Amazing Chesed: Living a Grace-Filled Judaism
By Rabbi Rami Shapiro Drawing from ancient and contemporary, traditional and non-traditional Jewish wisdom, reclaims the idea of grace in Judaism.
6 x 9, 176 pp, Quality PB, 978-1-58023-624-9 **$16.99**

Perennial Wisdom for the Spiritually Independent: Sacred Teachings—
Annotated & Explained Annotation by Rabbi Rami Shapiro; Foreword by Richard Rohr
Weaves sacred texts and teachings from the world's major religions into a coherent exploration of the five core questions at the heart of every religion's search.
5½ x 8½, 336 pp, Quality PB, 978-1-59473-515-8 **$16.99***

A Book of Life: Embracing Judaism as a Spiritual Practice
By Rabbi Michael Strassfeld 6 x 9, 544 pp, Quality PB, 978-1-58023-247-0 **$24.99**

Bringing the Psalms to Life: How to Understand and Use the Book of Psalms
By Rabbi Daniel F. Polish, PhD 6 x 9, 208 pp, Quality PB, 978-1-58023-157-2 **$18.99**

Does the Soul Survive? 2nd Edition: A Jewish Journey to Belief in Afterlife, Past Lives
& Living with Purpose By Rabbi Elie Kaplan Spitz; Foreword by Brian L. Weiss, MD
6 x 9, 288 pp, Quality PB, 978-1-58023-818-2 **$18.99**

First Steps to a New Jewish Spirit: Reb Zalman's Guide to Recapturing the Intimacy &
Ecstasy in Your Relationship with God By Rabbi Zalman Schachter-Shalomi (z"l) with Donald Gropman
6 x 9, 144 pp, Quality PB, 978-1-58023-182-4 **$16.95**

Foundations of Sephardic Spirituality: The Inner Life of Jews of the Ottoman Empire
By Rabbi Marc D. Angel, PhD 6 x 9, 224 pp, Quality PB, 978-1-58023-341-5 **$18.99**

The God Upgrade: Finding Your 21st-Century Spirituality in Judaism's 5,000-Year-
Old Tradition By Rabbi Jamie Korngold; Foreword by Rabbi Harold M. Schulweis
6 x 9, 176 pp, Quality PB, 978-1-58023-443-6 **$15.99**

The Jewish Lights Spirituality Handbook: A Guide to Understanding, Exploring &
Living a Spiritual Life Edited by Stuart M. Matlins
6 x 9, 456 pp, Quality PB, 978-1-58023-093-3 **$19.99**

Jewish with Feeling: A Guide to Meaningful Jewish Practice
By Rabbi Zalman Schachter-Shalomi (z"l) with Joel Segel
5½ x 8½, 288 pp, Quality PB, 978-1-58023-691-1 **$19.99**

Judaism, Physics and God: Searching for Sacred Metaphors in a Post-Einstein World
By Rabbi David W. Nelson
6 x 9, 352 pp, Quality PB, inc. reader's discussion guide, 978-1-58023-306-4 **$18.99**
HC, 352 pp, 978-1-58023-252-4 **$24.99**

Repentance: The Meaning and Practice of Teshuvah
By Dr. Louis E. Newman; Foreword by Rabbi Harold M. Schulweis; Preface by Rabbi Karyn D. Kedar
6 x 9, 256 pp, Quality PB, 978-1-58023-718-5 **$18.99**

Tanya, the Masterpiece of Hasidic Wisdom: Selections Annotated & Explained
Translation & Annotation by Rabbi Rami Shapiro; Foreword by Rabbi Zalman Schachter-Shalomi (z"l)
5½ x 8½, 240 pp, Quality PB, 978-1-59473-275-1 **$18.99***

These Are the Words, 2nd Edition: A Vocabulary of Jewish Spiritual Life
By Rabbi Arthur Green, PhD 6 x 9, 320 pp, Quality PB, 978-1-58023-494-8 **$19.99**

Your Word Is Fire: The Hasidic Masters on Contemplative Prayer
Edited and translated by Rabbi Arthur Green, PhD, and Barry W. Holtz
6 x 9, 160 pp, Quality PB, 978-1-879045-25-5 **$16.99**

*A book from SkyLight Paths, Jewish Lights' sister imprint

Meditation / Yoga

Increasing Wholeness: Jewish Wisdom & Guided Meditations to Strengthen & Calm Body, Heart, Mind & Spirit
By Rabbi Elie Kaplan Spitz Combines Jewish tradition, contemporary psychology and world spiritual writings with practical contemplative exercises to guide you to see the familiar in fresh new ways.
6 x 9, 208 pp, Quality PB, 978-1-58023-823-6 **$19.99**

Living the Life of Jewish Meditation: A Comprehensive Guide to Practice and Experience *By Rabbi Yoel Glick*
Combines the knowledge of Judaism with the spiritual practice of Yoga to lead you to an encounter with your true self. Includes nineteen different meditations.
6 x 9, 272 pp, Quality PB, 978-1-58023-802-1 **$18.99**

Mussar Yoga: Blending an Ancient Jewish Spiritual Practice with Yoga to Transform Body and Soul
By Edith R. Brotman, PhD, RYT-500; Foreword by Alan Morinis
A clear and easy-to-use introduction to an embodied spiritual practice for anyone seeking profound and lasting self-transformation.
7 x 9, 224 pp, 40+ b/w photos, Quality PB, 978-1-58023-784-0 **$18.99**

The Magic of Hebrew Chant: Healing the Spirit, Transforming the Mind, Deepening Love *By Rabbi Shefa Gold; Foreword by Sylvia Boorstein*
Introduces this transformative spiritual practice as a way to unlock the power of sacred texts and make prayer and meditation the delight of your life. Includes musical notations. 6 x 9, 352 pp, Quality PB, 978-1-58023-671-3 **$24.99**

The Magic of Hebrew Chant Companion: The Big Book of Musical Notations and Incantations 8½ x 11, 154 pp, PB, 978-1-58023-722-2 **$19.99**

Aleph-Bet Yoga: Embodying the Hebrew Letters for Physical and Spiritual Well-Being
By Steven A. Rapp; Foreword by Tamar Frankiel, PhD, and Judy Greenfeld; Preface by Hart Lazer
7 x 10, 128 pp, b/w photos, Quality PB, Lay-flat binding, 978-1-58023-162-6 **$16.95**

Discovering Jewish Meditation, 2nd Edition
Instruction & Guidance for Learning an Ancient Spiritual Practice
By Nan Fink Gefen, PhD 6 x 9, 208 pp, Quality PB, 978-1-58023-462-7 **$16.99**

The Handbook of Jewish Meditation Practices
A Guide for Enriching the Sabbath and Other Days of Your Life
By Rabbi David A. Cooper 6 x 9, 208 pp, Quality PB, 978-1-58023-102-2 **$16.95**

Jewish Meditation Practices for Everyday Life: Awakening Your Heart, Connecting with God By Rabbi Jeff Roth 6 x 9, 224 pp, Quality PB, 978-1-58023-397-2 **$18.99**

Ritual / Sacred Practices

God in Your Body: Kabbalah, Mindfulness and Embodied Spiritual Practice
By Jay Michaelson 6 x 9, 272 pp, Quality PB, 978-1-58023-304-0 **$18.99**

Jewish Ritual: A Brief Introduction for Christians
By Rabbi Kerry M. Olitzky and Rabbi Daniel Judson
5½ x 8½, 144 pp, Quality PB, 978-1-58023-210-4 **$14.99**

The Rituals & Practices of a Jewish Life: A Handbook for Personal Spiritual Renewal
Edited by Rabbi Kerry M. Olitzky and Rabbi Daniel Judson
6 x 9, 272 pp, Illus., Quality PB, 978-1-58023-169-5 **$19.99**

The Sacred Art of Lovingkindness: Preparing to Practice
By Rabbi Rami Shapiro 5½ x 8½, 176 pp, Quality PB, 978-1-59473-151-8 **$16.99***

Mystery & Detective Fiction

Criminal Kabbalah: An Intriguing Anthology of Jewish Mystery & Detective Fiction
Edited by Lawrence W. Raphael; Foreword by Laurie R. King
6 x 9, 256 pp, Quality PB, 978-1-58023-109-1 **$16.95**

Mystery Midrash: An Anthology of Jewish Mystery & Detective Fiction
Edited by Lawrence W. Raphael; Preface by Joel Siegel
6 x 9, 304 pp, Quality PB, 978-1-58023-055-1 **$16.95**

*A book from SkyLight Paths, Jewish Lights' sister imprint

About Jewish Lights

People of all faiths and backgrounds yearn for books that attract, engage, educate, and spiritually inspire.

Our principal goal is to stimulate thought and help all people learn about who the Jewish People are, where they come from, and what the future can be made to hold. While people of our diverse Jewish heritage are the primary audience, our books speak to people in the Christian world as well and will broaden their understanding of Judaism and the roots of their own faith.

We bring to you authors who are at the forefront of spiritual thought and experience. While each has something different to say, they all say it in a voice that you can hear.

Our books are designed to welcome you and then to engage, stimulate, and inspire. We judge our success not only by whether or not our books are beautiful and commercially successful, but by whether or not they make a difference in your life.

For your information and convenience, at the back of this book we have provided a list of other Jewish Lights books you might find interesting and useful. They cover all the categories of your life:

Bar/Bat Mitzvah	Life Cycle
Bible Study / Midrash	Meditation
Children's Books	Men's Interest
Congregation Resources	Parenting
Current Events / History	Prayer / Ritual / Sacred Practice
Ecology / Environment	Social Justice
Fiction: Mystery, Science Fiction	Spirituality
Grief / Healing	Theology / Philosophy
Holidays / Holy Days	Travel
Inspiration	Twelve Steps
Kabbalah / Mysticism / Enneagram	Women's Interest

Stuart M. Matlins, Publisher

Or phone, fax, mail or email to: **JEWISH LIGHTS Publishing**
Sunset Farm Offices, Route 4 • P.O. Box 237 • Woodstock, Vermont 05091
Tel: (802) 457-4000 • Fax: (802) 457-4004 • www.jewishlights.com
Credit card orders: **(800) 962-4544** (8:30AM–5:30PM EST Monday–Friday)
Generous discounts on quantity orders. SATISFACTION GUARANTEED. Prices subject to change.

For more information about each book, visit our website at www.jewishlights.com.